Singing the Lord's Song

in a Foreign Land

Singing the Lord's Song in a Foreign Land

Reclaiming Faith in a New Culture

Vivian Ligo

NOVALIS

© 2002 Novalis, Saint Paul University, Ottawa, Canada

Cover: Maria d.c. Zamora
Layout: Suzanne Latourelle

Business Office:
Novalis
49 Front Street East, 2nd Floor
Toronto, Ontario, Canada
M5E 1B3

Phone: 1-800-387-7164 or (416) 363-3303
Fax: 1-800-204-4140 or (416) 363-9409
E-mail: cservice@novalis.ca

National Library of Canada Cataloguing in Publication

Ligo, Vivian
    Singing the Lord's song in a foreign land : reclaiming faith in a new culture / Vivian Ligo.

Includes bibliographical references.
ISBN 2-89507-304-X

    1. Immigrants–Religious life. 2. Prayer–Catholic Church. 3. Emigration and immigration–Religious aspects–Catholic Church.
I. Title.

BV4596.E6L53 2002   248.3'2'08691   C2002-902977-5

Printed in Canada.

We acknowledge the financial support of the Government of Canada through the Book Publishing Industry Development Program (BPIDP) for our publishing activities.

10 9 8 7 6 5 4 3 2 1   10 09 08 07 06 05 04 03 02

Acknowledgments

*An immigrant's life story is a list of people
remembered and honoured with sincere gratitude.*

Bill Addley, S.J.
Stella Antoliago
The Benedicto family
John Boissonneau
The Boyd-Ralph family
David Buersmeyer and family
Kevin Burns
Raymond Collins
Maureen Coughlin, S.C.N.,
and the St. Agnes Community of S.C.N. Sisters
Patricia Coulter
Gordon Davies
Robert Foliot, S.J.
Bill German, S.J.
John Haught
Monika Hellwig
Michael Hutchins, S.V.D.
Veronica Koperski
Gemma Labitan and family
Tom and Janine Langan
James Maier
Mimi Marrocco
David Mellott and family
Ron Mercier, S.J.
Attila Miklósházy, S.J.
Bob Mulderig
Edit Nagy-Bakos
Armando Pertugia and family
The Proctor-Barrett family
The Ralph-Ahlers family
Maryam Rezai-Atrie
Hélène Royes
The Schmitz-Shropp family
Gerald Tait, S.J.
Stan Uroda, S.V.D.
Frank Volpini and family
Mary McSorley-Yake
&
My family here and back home

Contents

Introduction

To immigrate to another country is to move into a geography of loss, disorientation and hope for a homecoming in a foreign land. Letting go of a familiar way of life in anticipation of the unknown shapes such a landscape. Vulnerability alternating with numbness heightens the contrasts in the terrain. Traversing this place requires a certain openness that trembles with insecurity. The immigrant anticipates great things but remains naive about the toll this will take on the spirit.

The above words frame both the told and the untold narratives of immigrant life. A mere five sentences can bring forth a rush of memories that gives us immigrants pause. Between the lines lie tapestry upon tapestry of stories that we can weave with our own thread. Between the lines speak volumes about what may be left unspoken, yet told to ourselves, conveyed in silent understanding as we allow the words to sink in.

The immigrant experience can provoke a faith crisis. Two related questions drawn from the Bible express this well: "My God, my God, why have you forsaken me?" (Psalm 22:1) and "How could we sing the LORD's song in a foreign land?" (Psalm 137:4). To seek an answer to these questions, I turn to the biblical theology of exile. In the prophets Jeremiah, Ezekiel and Second Isaiah (Isaiah 40–55), I find a spiritual home. I find a theological language for my soul.

What I write, then, is a prayerful reflection on the immigrant experience.[1] But though this reflection has autobiographical elements, it is not essentially an autobiography. It invites you, the reader, to add your own stories. Reading the text may lead you to self-knowledge and intimacy with your own immigrant life. Though I attempt to make Jeremiah, Ezekiel and Second Isaiah accessible, I do not pretend to offer a detailed scholarly exegesis, or interpretation. I invite you to pray in, with and through the prophets of exile. Though I offer some prayers, I cannot pray on your behalf. I chart instead a process of praying that you may undertake in order to engage in your experience.

Though I offer vignettes of my life, I am more intent on demonstrating a way to meet the God of exile, the God of Jeremiah, Ezekiel and Second Isaiah. I draw a spiritual cartography of an immigrant soul. What is set before you is a theological map-making that opens a seemingly forbidding terrain to prayerful passage. I invite you to take a similar journey, where you may encounter your self and find yourself in a place where God may choose to reveal God's own self.[2]

This spiritual exercise may have significance for the Church. No longer central to most people's lives, the Church is in exile and may be able to learn from Jeremiah, Ezekiel and Second Isaiah. As well, the theology of exile speaks to other experiences of displacement. It is not only the immigrant who feels displaced today.

As immigrant life becomes the landscape for reflection, immigrants may discover that they can identify each turn with their own story. An immigrant's story can be uneventful, or it can be dramatic, conflicted, filled with adventure, fraught with risks and challenges, and racked with heartbreaking dissonances.

Though specifics of time, origin, motivations, surrounding circumstances and emotional undercurrents vary, and though the telling of the stories may not be factually straightforward, all our particularities will convey beyond words what immigrant life entails.

A personal vignette

In 1990, after marrying a Canadian, I left the Philippines to join him in Washington, D.C. Two years later, with a newborn daughter in tow, we moved to Toronto. My application for landed immigrant status began in the Philippines. The immigration officer required that I provide her with proofs of personal correspondence between my husband and me. I complied, though I felt it was a blatant intrusion into my personal life. One interview question asked whether I eventually planned to sponsor my immediate family to move to Canada. I answered no. With my departure for the U.S., the application began again, this time in Washington, D.C. It moved through the usual bureaucratic maze. Once it was approved, I was finally considered a legitimate member of Canadian society.

My situation drew me to prayer. Perhaps because of my cultural background and introspective temperament, coupled with my theological training and profession, I have found praying to be the safest place to come to terms with my experiences.

To me, praying is not merely a habit, like brushing my teeth. Neither is it merely mumbling formulas absent-mindedly. It is placing myself in the presence of God. I converse with God, address God, pouring out everything that I am and disposing myself wholly to God's graciousness.

This prayerful posture is physical: I sit straight, close my eyes, breathe naturally, deeply, rhythmically, while relaxing all areas of my body that are tense and weighed down. It is metaphysical: I assume that beyond the material and the sensible is a larger, grace-filled, ultimate, divine and holy reality whom I can address and who in turn responds, or better, who addresses me and waits for my response. It is pneumatological: I invoke the Holy Spirit to come help me pray. It is creedal: I consciously ask that I be grounded in the mystery of the incarnation and resurrection of Jesus. It is psychological: I pay attention to my interior reality, wherein I acknowledge and bring to prayer those with whom I am emotionally bound, such as my own family. It is visceral: I acknowledge the deep sources of my anxiety and desire, and let all these ascend unto the LORD. It is intercessory: I bring to prayer specific individuals who cross my path, and whose own burdens and woes I also seem to feel. I surrender them to God. I offer my work and the people to whom I minister. I invoke Mary, the Blessed Mother, all the angels and saints, to be there with me in prayer.

Praying is verbal and mental: I utter prayers again and again, repeating them like a mantra, as I keep on releasing thoughts and feelings. Praying is also imaginative: I dwell in biblical scenes, so that I can linger in this prayerful mode attentively and openly, in word and beyond word. After a time, my eyes open of their own accord. I end the ritual with the sign of the cross. Then I move on with the day and live it as it comes.

Implicit in this prayerful posture is a religious world view. In 1986, while I pursued a doctorate in Religious Studies at the Catholic University of Louvain, in Belgium, I composed a personal interpretation of the Christian creed. I find that it still articulates my religious convictions.

I believe in God…
Before I conclude intelligently, I already intuit that before me, around me, under me, after me, I am confronted, enfolded, supported, summoned by something-someone larger than myself.

Because of this intuition I organize all my experiences and the experiences of the world into a meaningful pattern. I begin to be conscious that I am part of a chain of events whose beginnings go back into a distant past (I call it primordial) and whose completion is stretched into a distant future (I call it eternity).

This chain of events is a story. There is conflict that must be resolved. There is openness to surprises, tragic or otherwise. There is discovery. There are questions, crying and laughing, play and celebration, tedious repetition, boredom and pain. And always there are people. There is community. There is the human world.

Once in a while I apprehend this larger-than-myself, this larger-than-the-human world piercing through my eyes into my inner eye, which sees and recognizes this as the IS — ineluctable, immense, working in its own good time, so true, so beautiful, so right. I am in for an adventure in thought, in feeling, in life. Every concrete experience is the datum for such an adventure. And always there is the desire to pierce through each datum, to take it apart in order to coax out of it some glimpse of the IS, some touch with reality.

…the Father almighty, creator of heaven and earth…

The IS is not indifferent. It is warm, inviting, revealing and responding. It plays. It listens. It wants to be recognized, affirmed and danced to. It enjoys the company of its creation. It finds its home in intelligibility and feeling. It finds its home in me — in my human cognition and mental representation, in my words: Father, Creator of heaven and earth.

Father: Life-giving, protecting, teaching, disciplining, home-beckoning, just like mother.

Almighty: outpouring generously, summoning all that I am wholly into its grasp, into its presence.

Creator of heaven and earth: allowing limitless possibilities, giving freedom, exacting responsibility.

…and in Jesus Christ, his only Son, our Lord, who was conceived by the power of the Holy Spirit, born of the Virgin Mary, suffered under Pontius Pilate, was crucified, died, and was buried.

One of its original ideas is to take human life seriously, to take the human way of journeying and coming home, to become human in Jesus. Even suffering, evil and death are not alien to it anymore. It must love stories so much that it joins in the conflict, the surprise, the tragedy, the happy ending.

Being human is the way to transcendence. Being rooted is the way to soar; being crucified is the way to freedom.

Being human is the way to discover how reality works and how human lives can work if attentiveness is lent to this reality.

Human life is the river delta where reality and human constructions converge paradoxically.

I resolve to live human life deeply.

He descended to the dead. On the third day he rose again. He ascended into heaven and sits at the right hand of God. He will come again to judge the living and the dead…

I resolve to live human life deeply because the IS has taken it so seriously; our human way may not be so far removed from its ways. The very mystery of reality is right there in the most ordinary, the most mundane and the most human.

I believe in the Holy Spirit, the Lord, the giver of life, who proceeds from the Father and the Son. With the Father and the Son he is worshipped and glorified…

I resolve – because even prior to my intuition I have been, after all, called to see life this way – to proceed through life's ambiguities this way, for I am part of this constant and ever-changing, open-ended wholeness – this sky, this sea, this heart.

Therefore, I believe in God, the Father, the Son and the Holy Spirit. I believe in God's ebbing and flowing, God's movement to a destiny that is mine, too, God's being named and namelessness, God's now here-ness and nowhere-ness.

I believe that the very human experience that comes closest to God's Trinitarian nature is love. When I love, I become lover. The one I love, the beloved, makes me a beloved, and we rejoice in the strength of love that invites us to love some more. Who called the lover to love? What made the beloved respond? Why is this mystery so close and yet so expansive it draws the human heart inside out?

I believe in the holy catholic Church, the communion of saints, the forgiveness of sins, the resurrection of the body and the life everlasting. Amen.

I believe in myself. I believe in other creatures — human and non-human. I posit in them my trust, though I have known betrayals, for there is no other world in which life becomes indeed an adventure and a challenge.

I believe in the meaningfulness of life. I trust in its goodness. I expect its happy ending.

And I am willing to pay the price for it all. Amen.

Taking Christianity, and more specifically the Roman Catholic tradition, as essentially mediating a personal relationship with God in Jesus, I am drawn to pursue and savour its depths not only intellectually but also personally. I appreciate it beyond its seemingly stringent rules that have made some people miserable, beyond its institutionalized devotional practices that channel sentimental and pious feelings, beyond its definitions that are wrongly taken as resolving all of life's ambiguities. If lived more deeply, the Roman Catholic tradition ceases to appear as a narrow-minded stance that looks down on unbelievers, or as a relic of a pre-scientific era that refuses to go away.

The Roman Catholic tradition is a particular and historical expression of God's participation in our life. It makes present within the community of believers the revelation that God became a human being in Jesus, and that the most appropriate access to this God is a personal relationship. It is by far more engaging, truer to its essence and more fruitful to plumb its depths from within than to attempt to establish objective criteria by which to judge its claim to possess the absolute revelation of God. Therefore, when I pray, I seek depth.

The vicissitudes of immigrant life changed my personal landscape, but I never consciously decided to craft a prayerful reflection. I simply prayed. Though immigrant by choice, I underestimated the external and internal changes that would be required of me. But I prayed and proceeded with day-to-day living.

Raising the theological question

More often than not, when I find myself mirrored in others, creative ways of dealing with my own situation become apparent. Invited in 1995 to join the Board of Trustees of a college seminary in Epworth, Iowa, I saw much more starkly how central the immigrant experience is to an immigrant's new sense of self, of God, of the future, and of his or her place in a foreign country. About 85 per cent of Divine Word College Seminary's students were Vietnamese; the rest were Hispanic, Caribbean, Chinese, Filipino, and Irish- and Polish-American. Perched on a small hill in white, middle-class rural Iowa, the seminary's unique profile raised a question: "Why not use the immigrant background of the students as the locus for their formation?"

Thus began a research project that has spoken to me in a strikingly personal way. My research has become an ongoing reflection that has brought me to different levels of conversation with the formation team of the college seminary, with other immigrants, with myself, with God, with students, with those who minister to immigrants, with religious communities, with biblical texts, and with scholarly interpretations of biblical texts.

Writing this prayerful reflection has been just one part of this continuing conversation. The link between the immigrant experience and the biblical theology of exile is not obvious. Theoretical discussions occur even before the insight can begin to enchant and captivate the imagination.

A budding immigrant biblical scholar interjects that diaspora is a better term than "exile" for the immigrant situation. I fail to persuade her that, nevertheless, the sound of the word "exile" captures the longing, the loneliness, the homesickness that can unexpectedly visit immigrants even if they are eager to leave their homeland. Diaspora is technically correct, but lacks the suggestive, evocative and echoing tonality of the word "exile."

An immigrant priest similarly objects to the use of the biblical theology of exile because the immigrants he meets are quite happy to be in their country of adoption. Whereas the exiled in the Bible are promised a return to their homeland, immigrants, for the most part, have decided to remain in their new country.

A particularly difficult group in one parish insists that I lecture only on the spirituality of the prophets of exile, without reference to immigrants. This group, which is primarily of Irish and Italian descent, no longer finds immigrant issues relevant despite the fact that their pastor of four years is a Filipino immigrant, and about 45 other, more recently landed, ethnic groups can be found in the parish.

Interest in the fit between the immigrant experience and the biblical theology of exile wanes when people realize it involves effort to change and redirect their approach to Scripture, prayer and consequent religious formation.

I have also encountered resistance to the whole prospect of prayer – or, if not resistance, incomprehension. It is much easier to talk about a research project than to lead people towards a theological appropriation through prayer. Offering to pray on their behalf or for another person is more welcome than inviting them to pray through their own immigrant experience. The resistance sometimes changes to defiance when praying begins with Jeremiah.

I belong to a multi-ethnic parish in downtown Toronto. Most of the parishioners are Filipinos, but the parish is not exclusively Filipino. Newcomers are struck by the hospitality and friendliness of Our Lady of Lourdes Parish. Even if no one knows their name, they feel they belong.

More than that, the pastors and their pastoral teams convey that they know the plight of the parishioners. They know highly qualified immigrants who are stalled in their job search because the basic requirement is Canadian work experience. They know mothers who have left their own families to work as nannies here, raising someone else's children. They know lonely men and women working three or four jobs so they can send money back home. They know frustrated grandparents who feel isolated living in high-rise apartments as their children and grandchildren "do their own thing." Marriages break down because familiar support systems are non-existent here. There are uneasy compromises as families reunite after years of separation, and find themselves unable to really connect.

Our Lady of Lourdes Parish twice allowed me to walk the congregation through praying the immigrant experience as exile. The first time, I led a two-and-a-half hour Bible study session each Sunday for three weeks, on Jeremiah, Ezekiel and Second Isaiah. The second time, I gave a three-evening Lenten retreat.

In the Bible study sessions, we begin with our immigrant story, mindful that though our own is unique, it also has something in common with the stories of others. Aware that not everyone may be comfortable sharing their personal experience in a group setting, I use a movie, *Pushing Hands,* as a starting point. *Pushing Hands* is about a Chinese T'ai Chi master who comes to America to join his son's family. The culture clash begins in the home with his son's American wife.

The discussions that follow afterward focus on the movie, while implicitly referring to each one of us and our own unique situation. We all know this, but we are grateful for the shield of anonymity. As we configure a shared experience, we insert ourselves in a reflection that takes its cue from the biblical theology of exile. We learn from biblical scholars about the text, but rely more on our own willingness to be led to prayer.

In the Lenten retreat, I follow the structure of the Liturgy of the Word. Through proclamation of the word, shared reflection, songs and symbolic acts, the parishioners ritualize the act of commending their immigrant experiences into God's hands. They discover meaning as their lives are cradled by God's word. They unknowingly become theologians of their own destiny.

Prayer as context for theologizing

Only prayerful reflection, shared or private, can offer a way of fully personalizing the biblical theology of exile. Any other way falls short of such a potential. I have offered the construct as an elective course at the Toronto School of Theology. I have delivered it as a paper in an academic conference. I have written a short article for a journal. I have introduced it to communities of priests and religious. Yet, if this personalization of the biblical theology of exile stays at the level of discussion and does not move into prayerful appropriation, the distance created removes the immigrant from the benefits and hazards of a fuller engagement.

To interpret our immigrant experience as exile is to locate our self at its heart, and there pray with Jeremiah, Ezekiel and Second Isaiah. By so doing, our immigrant experience is no longer in the background of, but is central to, our continuous attempt to understand the ways of the Lord in our life as an individual and as a member of a community. We do not have to be a Catholic to enter into this event of prayerful dialogue with Scripture. If you are not a Christian, you may explore your own tradition, if you wish to place your immigrant situation within the context of prayer.

Praying requires total participation and performance. When we no longer pray by rote or by mindlessly chattering, but become engaged in dialogue with Scripture, prayer can be daunting. It asks for honest openness of the mind, heart and depth of our being. It is a spiritual event that enables us to live our total reality, including its difficult and painful aspects.

True prayer takes place within a framework of dialogue. Uttering certain prayers is merely a beginning. True prayer happens when we really mean what we pray, from our mind but also from our heart and from our gut. We move from word to silence, from the superficial to the truly deep, from being partially present to God to becoming totally gathered before God. There are prayers and there is prayer. It is into the latter that I invite you to venture.

A Prayer Refrain

And so let us pray as we put ourselves at the heart of our immigrant condition:

By the rivers of Babylon –
there we sat down and there we wept
when we remembered Zion.
On the willows there
we hung up our harps.
For there our captors
asked us for songs,
and our tormentors asked for mirth, saying,
"Sing us one of the songs of Zion!"
How could we sing the LORD's song
in a foreign land?

(Psalm 137:1–4)

I invite you to be grateful to your host country for its hospitality to immigrants and the displaced. I ask you to be forgiving in the face of experiences of racism and discrimination. Let us pray:

> By the rivers of Babylon –
> there we sat down and there we wept
> when we remembered Zion.
> On the willows there
> we hung up our harps.
> For there our captors
> asked us for songs,
> and our tormentors asked for mirth, saying,
> "Sing us one of the songs of Zion!"
> How could we sing the LORD's song
> in a foreign land?
> *(Psalm 137:1–4)*

Consider fellow immigrants and those they have left behind in their country of birth. Let us pray:

> By the rivers of Babylon –
> there we sat down and there we wept
> when we remembered Zion.
> On the willows there
> we hung up our harps.
> For there our captors
> asked us for songs,
> and our tormentors asked for mirth, saying,
> "Sing us one of the songs of Zion!"
> How could we sing the LORD's song
> in a foreign land?
> *(Psalm 137:1–4)*

Carry in your heart millions and millions of refugees who, right now, are fleeing their homelands: people from Guatemala, El Salvador, Nicaragua, Surinam, Colombia, Haiti; people from Mauritania, Western Sahara, Mali, Senegal, Sierra Leone, Liberia, Togo, Angola, Zaire, South Africa, Mozambique, Burundi, Rwanda, Uganda, Ethiopia, Eritrea, Somalia, Sudan, Chad; people from Palestine, Iraq, Iran, Tajikistan, Bhutan, Afghanistan; people from Sri Lanka, Cambodia, Indonesia, Laos, Vietnam, Bangladesh, Myanmar, Tibet; people from Yugoslavia, Croatia. Let us pray:

> By the rivers of Babylon –
> there we sat down and there we wept
> when we remembered Zion.
> On the willows there
> we hung up our harps.
> For there our captors
> asked us for songs,
> and our tormentors asked for mirth, saying,
> "Sing us one of the songs of Zion!"
> How could we sing the LORD's song
> in a foreign land?
> *(Psalm 137:1–4)*

Linger awhile in a quiet space within yourself. Say a prayer of faith and trust. If you can sing, sing a song of trust. If all you can do is hum a hymn, then hum.

Do something very concrete for someone who is having trouble "singing the LORD's song in a foreign land."

This prayer has a story of its own. Prayed for the first time at one of the Our Lady of Lourdes Parish Bible study sessions, it drew the participants from simply reciting it together to really praying it together. They understood, without being able to fully articulate it, that the psalm was their prayer too, even with its very biblical imagery and feel. In another setting, a group of immigrant priests who minister in the archdiocese of Toronto objected to this prayer: first, to its application to the lives of immigrants, and second, to its usefulness in addressing immigrant issues in a parish. In the academic setting, this prayer goes unnoticed, a mere pedagogical tool to bring together Scripture and contemporary experience.

Christian tradition teaches that Scripture has two levels of meaning, the literal and the spiritual. The spiritual entails a move from the allegorical to the moral, and then to the anagogical. The literal is how the text reads. Modern readers can include on this level what scholars tell us about the text. The spiritual is the deeper and more important meaning: the allegorical involves placing ourselves as the real characters acting in relation to God; the moral involves the call to conversion; and the anagogical brings the reader before God, whose presence all the while has been mediated by the text.

Praying Psalm 137:1–4, for instance, uses the psalm as a text that speaks for us before God. That is why it is crucial that we allow the text to come to life not only in the mind, but also in our heart and deep in our being. Repeating the prayer more than once helps us descend into our depth, while at the same time enlarging the circumference of our concern. No matter how private and intimately personal prayer is, it carries with itself the summons to also care for others.

After everything has been uttered, we linger in prayer. As we remain silent yet totally present to God, contemplation begins and we reach the anagogical threshold. When we consciously act on what we pray, the integral connection between prayer and ministry is restored.

You may wish to go back to the prayer refrain so that you can both inhabit it more fully and allow the text to lead you closer to God.

This book, therefore, is not something you can gobble up in one sitting. At some point, you may be tempted to put it down, because it requires considerable self-investment. The words and insights you read here may strike too close for comfort. They will ask you to self-reveal when instinctively you will wish to duck. Then, when you do courageously face the many dimensions of your own particular immigrant experience, you will be led to prayer.

Even those who believe in God may have an ambivalent relationship with prayer. Prayer may be a pleasant memory of childhood, later altered by adult knowing and yet now may seem far beyond retrieval. Prayer might be a mere cognitive exercise or a mouthing of approved pious phrases that are quite distant from where wordlessly seethe the raw issues of life, meaning, faith, doubt and destiny. Prayer might have become a mere routine, and therefore, useless and ineffective in creating change.

I have worked on this construct for years. I have listened to immigrants tell their stories. I have read about very moving and lyrical renditions of the same experience. I have watched movies that dramatize its inherent tragedy and comedy. What I write is my way of honouring all these stories. I see myself in them, and I hope to proclaim the God I have met in mine.

Suggested readings

André Aciman, ed. *Letters of Transit*. New York: The New Press, 1999.

Milly Charon, ed. *Between Two Worlds: The Canadian Immigrant Experience*. Dunvegan, Ontario: Quadrant Editions, 1983.

Thomas Dublin, ed. *Immigrant Voices, 1773–1986*. Urbana and Chicago: University of Illinois Press, 1993.

Eva Hoffman. *Lost in Translation: A Life in a New Language*. New York: Penguin Books, 1989.

Jade Ngoc Quang Huynh. *South Wind Changing*. St. Paul, MN: Graywolf Press, 1994.

Thomas Kessner and Betty Boyd Caroli, eds. *Today's Immigrants, Their Stories: A New Look at the Newest Americans*. New York: Oxford University Press, 1981.

Elizabeth Kim. *Ten Thousand Sorrows*. Toronto: Doubleday, 2000.

Wendy Lowenstein and Morag Loh. *The Immigrants*. Melbourne: Hyland House, 1977.

Frank McCourt. *'Tis*. New York: Scribner, 1999.

Jube Namias. *First Generation: In the Words of Twentieth-Century American Immigrants*. Urbana and Chicago: University of Illinois Press, 1978.

Rodel J. Ramos. *In Search of a Future: The Struggle of Immigrants*. Toronto: RJRamos Enterprise, 1994.

Thomas C. Wheeler, ed. *The Immigrant Experience: The Anguish of Becoming American*. New York: The Dial Press, 1971.

The following films also depict the immigrant condition:
- *Alamo Bay*
- *Between Heaven and Earth*
- *Bread and Chocolate*
- *Broken English*
- *Crossings*
- *Double Happiness*
- *El Norte*
- *Floating Life*
- *Jerusalem*
- *Journey of Hope*
- *The Joy Luck Club*
- *Kolya*
- *Milk and Honey*
- *Mississippi Masala*
- *Not Without My Daughter*
- *Pushing Hands*
- *Snow Falling on Cedars*
- *A Thousand Pieces of Gold*

Laying Down
the Spiritual Landscape

Most of us can trace our beginnings to immigrants. Throughout history, waves of immigrants have moved to other countries in the hope that life will be better there. Some succeed. Others do not. Some become part of mainstream culture in their adopted home. Others remain on the periphery. Later generations forget their immigrant beginnings. Others are always reminded that they "do not really come from here."

The crisis of loss, disorientation and the hope for a homecoming

Experts say that immigrants face the twofold crisis of loss and overload. What these experts know through research, we know by experience deep in our bones. Because we immigrate, we lose home, homeland, family, friends, work, social status, material possessions, identity and self-esteem. Without these components of our familiar world, we also lose our bearings and a certain unthinking naturalness with which we have related to our immediate surroundings. Something inside tenses up and holds back, suspiciously watching, never totally abandoning itself to spontaneous self-expression. There is always a part of us that cannot join the dance.

We translate ourselves into another language. Though we may already have some fluency, we betray ourselves with our thick accents, with our faulty diction. Though it is now unspoken, our native language still reveals itself in the inability of our facial muscles to enunciate English words properly. As we speak, we helplessly witness native English speakers straining to comprehend as they listen to us.

Languages collide and hang suspended in mid-air for want of easy translation. The Filipino national language and its many regional dialects, for example, have only one pronoun to refer to both the male and the female genders. Before we can catch ourselves, we use "her" instead of "him," or "he" instead of "she," "hers" instead of "his." We only have one preposition for "in," "on," "upon," "to," "of," "into," "against," "at," "within." Why are there so many prepositions in English? Of course, a native English speaker could retort, "Why do you only have one?"

We place accents on the wrong syllables. We render into English some local idioms but fail to preserve their meaning. English as a Second Language (ESL) teachers in the Philippines tell us that we will know we have mastered English if we dream in it. Not true. When we are very tired or very angry, English words evaporate from our memory, and our tongue, moulded in our native language, takes the reins. Conversely, when we hear angry English expletives, they never seem to insult as painfully as our own expletives do.

Worse than losing the opportunity to use our language is losing our bearings in terms of how to relate to people. Our inner barometer that registers friendliness cannot read another person's distant politeness. Coming from a culture that puts a premium on hospitality, we gauge our worthiness, acceptability and likeability in terms of how another person makes us feel at home. It does not occur to us that it is our responsibility to achieve such a comfort level on our own. It does not occur to us that smiling shyly leads nowhere.

Smiling goes a long way in the Philippines. It is recognition of the other. It establishes familiarity. After a few encounters, we begin to chat, and perhaps, on the third or fourth meeting, we get to know each other's names. The opposite happens here. People must know your name first before they acknowledge that they have met you. You may cross paths regularly. You exchange passing glances. You smile. The other stares back. The first time you join in conversation, they ask, "Excuse me, have we met before?"

It takes a while to realize that in North America, "How are you?" is a greeting, not a question. I suppose the Filipino way of greeting one another in the street might be a jolt for people here. Although we have Filipinized the Spanish *como esta* (how are you?) into *kumusta*, culturally we add the question, "Where are you going?" Transposed to a different culture and language, the question appears somewhat nosy.

I come from a culture whose articulation of itself is part linguistic and part sublinguistic. We communicate through the raising of our eyebrows, through a certain look, a narrowing or meaningful downcast turn of the eye or surreptitious glance, through the set of our mouth when we smile, through an inflection in our voice. This sublinguistic realm is laden with emotional undercurrents that we wordlessly decode to avoid direct confrontation. Our silence is filled with meaning. Even before the other has spoken, we have listened for signals of openness and welcome. When no such signals come, we lose some sense of a habitable world.

This complex web of unspoken emotional exchange is only one facet of a habitable world; it is also constructed in space. In the Philippines, we tend to occupy space with bodily presence. We do not mind having to share a bed, much less a bedroom, crowded though we might be. We have no direct translation for the English word "privacy."

There is so much space here. Canada is vast. Canada is sheer space, and native-born Canadians tend to claim it not only physically, but also personally. They must have their space. To require so much space for one's self seems to me to create loneliness. But for those who prize it, space is freedom. Invade that space, and one becomes a weighty and annoying encumbrance.

We also tend to work around an encumbrance. We bend and sway like a pliant bamboo. We do not firmly stand our ground, nor do we engage in conflict with those who stand in our way. By default we give in when people dig in their heels or when they become adversarial in order to brand their will on situations. It takes a few cognitive shifts for us to override this default and deal with these situations effectively. We learn the hard way that silently sulking does not work.

A habitable world also consists of a sense of time. Where I come from, we experience time as cyclic. Nothing is really lost to the past. What goes, comes back. We languidly live the present moment. We enjoy it. We entrust our future to fate or to the providence of God. We do not have the psychic mechanism to cope with a culture that wants to manipulate the future with its schedules, forecasts and strategies. It is quite amazing to me that what seems to be a hazy, yet-to-come future actually submits to human programming.

And there is a sense of rhythm in my homeland. Everyone is in a rush here. Life becomes a blur. The fastest way is the best way. Multi-tasking is the norm. Harassed, I see myself in Garfield, the cat, plastered on a car window.

A habitable world is sensate. I associate certain sounds with home: honking vehicles, blaring radios, loud karaoke singalongs, arguing neighbours, screaming kids that wake you up and accompany you to sleep. Here in Canada you can call the police to complain about noise. The world I come from has certain smells, like fried rice and salted fish for breakfast. These foods not only stink here, but they also leave their stink in the room, on clothing, on the drapes for days. My world is of the palate, a homey fondness for saltiness and sourness. I must learn not to extravagantly sprinkle salt and soy sauce on the food I prepare. Homesickness is visceral. I often crave Filipino food, and am satisfied only after I heartily partake of it. I have a constant supply of Asian (not Uncle Ben's) rice at home.

Who and how to touch are encoded differently in the Philippines. We do not shake hands when introduced to another. We smile and nod our heads in acknowledgment. We lavish hugs and kisses on children but the frequency decreases as they grow older. Lovers do not kiss openly. They seek anonymity in dark movie theatres or parks. Teaching for two years in a high school in Toronto, I saw teenaged lovers freely express intimacy in such unlikely places as the corridor or the locker area or the staircase. I looked away in embarrassment.

Back home, we never talk much about the weather. It is either too hot, or too wet, or too stormy to be a topic of conversation. But when I visit, everyone asks me how winter feels and what snow is like. Snow is part of the enchantment of going abroad. In the Philippines, at Christmas time, we install artificial Christmas trees decked with cotton balls or soapsuds to simulate snow. "White Christmas" is part of our carolling repertoire. I remember my childlike glee when I saw my first snow. I wrote a letter home describing it as sugar or cotton balls falling from the sky and settling on the ground.

As we lose our former sense of the world, we begin to orient ourselves to an unfamiliar one. With compelling pressures to survive, find work, express ourselves in a foreign tongue, we struggle to develop new sets of sensors by which to navigate a changed environment.

Skills mastered in the old world seem to be irrelevant in the new. Skills the new world requires are harder to learn. In new situations, we feel as though we have two left feet, or that we need to produce a third foot because our own are still rooted in our former world. Uprooted, we struggle to reroot ourselves towards new growth here. In the rerooting, we cope with stress, even with trauma, hoping that we will take to the soil.

If I were a brilliant astrophysicist, fluent in many computer languages, I might have easily found a job in some high-tech lab. Holding a Ph.D. in Religious Studies in the Roman Catholic tradition did not exactly make me a sought-after commodity. My graduate degree limited me to educational institutions, and more specifically, to Roman Catholic institutions. Although I never enjoyed the cold calls and appointments I had to make with deans or heads of theology departments, I did them anyway, with a tight knot in my stomach. I received both friendly and unfriendly responses. Two female academics perfunctorily suggested that I try teaching high school. According to them, there was no place for me in higher education.

As immigrants, we feel at times that our whole being is caught between a door and the door jamb because there seems to be no opportunity for us in this new world. At other times we feel we must assume a bigger role on a bigger stage, when previously we have known only bit parts on a smaller one. Or, we might have left home feeling like big fish in a small pond, only to find ourselves a puny fish in a much larger pond. We alternate between a sense of loss and hope, between hope and disorientation, between disorientation and homesickness, between "making it" and missing something. We vacillate between feeling now here and nowhere.

Not to be deterred, I tried agencies as another route towards employment. Armed with a basic knowledge of WordPerfect and Lotus, I revised my résumé to suit the business culture. I was sent on assignments and felt elated when managers requested me to work for them again.

I was lucky to eventually be employed where my academic qualifications can be put to use: I teach theology at St. Augustine's Seminary of the Toronto School of Theology. But I was an unemployed Ph.D. the first year after I left the Philippines, employed part-time in the second, stringing part-time teaching jobs in my third year, and then granted a full-time teaching position at the seminary in the fourth.

A colleague finds it strange that I consider myself lucky. She has the reverse view: the seminary is lucky to have her. But being Caucasian, born and raised Canadian, she does not know what it means to be an immigrant, what it means to be an outsider trying to get in, what it means to face an unseen and impenetrable cultural wall that keeps a person out. Immigrants do not wish simply to get in. We also wish to stay with a good measure of respectability, the kind we used to know. And that does not always happen.

Even with my luck, I have not been spared the experience of straddling two worlds. Shocked by new and pressing demands, we immigrants tend to hold on to some source of security, whether it is our native music, native food, native newspapers and movies, friends of the same ethnic background or cultural religious practices. We hold on to fragments of home, while we ride the flood of the new and unfamiliar. We cannot stop it from infiltrating.

The place of in-betweenness

Most of us experience leaving our country as an exodus, only to find that we have ended up in exile. We expect life to be better, and yet are shocked by the reality of struggle. While fascinated with the best aspects of our host country, we are also disheartened by its worst aspects. We send to our families and

33

friends countless photographs of all the tourist attractions we have visited. And on our own, we try to take in stride regular doses of racism and discrimination. Both fascinating and disheartening, our new world continually spreads its net over us. The old world still resides in our memory, and it powerfully influences our adjustment. During the day, we inhabit the world of the now. At night, in solitude, in dreams, in pangs of homesickness, we return to the world of our past.

When we actually revisit our mother country, we find, to our dismay, that it is no longer home either. We have become strangers in our own land. Feelings of disdain for it – it is too slow, too hot, too dusty, too undisciplined, too inefficient, too backward, and too impervious to change – actually jolt us. We pine for the clean, orderly and efficient life of our country of adoption. Reconnecting with friends and family back home becomes very trying. Life has essentially remained the same for them. We cannot claim that placidity for ourselves.

When a parent dies, a deeper kind of severance from the old country takes place. Future visits there cease to be homecoming. When my mother called to break the news about my father's death from cancer, I felt like my entrails were wrenched from me. Unable to cry at first, I lit a vigil candle.

Only after five years of living in Canada did I lose my self-consciousness about not being Caucasian. Yet even now, as I circulate among Caucasian Canadians, I am asked, albeit diplomatically, how long I have lived in Canada. Of course, my accent gives me away. I chat with a Canadian whose husband is a lawyer. I ask in what area her husband specializes. She enumerates them, and then adds, looking straight into my eyes, that she regrets her husband does not handle immigration cases.

I find myself in places where Third World immigrants are working behind the service counter, not sitting down to be served. They look at me as though I am on the wrong side of the counter – the same way Caucasian customers glance at me.

Once when I was waiting with my daughter at a yacht club for her sailing lessons to begin, I offered friendly overtures to one of the mothers. She stared at me with utter surprise, informed me that in the afternoon her Filipina nanny would pick up her daughter, and promptly turned her back to me. Even among my own people, I am mistaken for my daughter's nanny. I am reminded, intentionally or unintentionally, that I do not really belong here.

As immigrants, we inhabit an in-between world, and find ourselves homeless. We can feel trapped and live in quiet desperation. Without some hope of a homecoming, we run the risk of becoming violently self-destructive, or being closed in upon by our own ethnic group, or "crossing over to the other side," so that we become more Canadian than Canadians. Or, we can live in both worlds, taking the culture clash as it comes, swallowing inconsistencies that are bearable, and forging on. I have witnessed our ability to do this. Once, at a Filipino socio-religious event, I was quite amazed by how we all sang both the Canadian and the Filipino national anthems with the same fervour, enthusiasm and sincerity.

The clash of cultures

Crossing over to another culture is never simple. Immigration officers at any border make sure that this is our first lesson. A brown Filipino passport seems to trigger, in an almost Pavlovian sense, an aggressiveness on their part that forces silent acquiescence on ours. Mental, emotional, attitudinal, motivational, psychological and behavioural shifts begin thus. Immigrants are regarded as intruders who must prove themselves to be legally allowed entry to the country. We cannot swagger over-assertively because, though the officers cannot refuse us entry, they can make us wait a long time for our passports to be processed. We do not want to be too friendly because these immigration officers do not reciprocate such displays of familiarity. We try to stay calm and cool because any sign of nervousness will make them suspicious. As we wait longer in line, we gradually lose our composure. The confidence exuded in a "heads up, shoulders relaxed, chest out, stomach in" posture slowly disappears into a defeated, slouching, pathetic look.

Being impeded at the borders because of my Filipino passport finally prodded me to seek Canadian citizenship. Travelling on one occasion to Washington, D.C., for a visit – my husband with his Canadian passport, our daughter with her American passport, and me with a Filipino passport thick with landed immigrant documents – we were taken aside by immigration officials for routine interrogation: Who was my employer in Toronto? What did we intend to do in Washington? When were we returning to Toronto?

Though culture is human-made, it takes on the force of second nature. All of us, human beings, experience its gravitational pull instinctively. We discover differences when our built-in responses to events and circumstances clash with the built-in expectations of another culture. Our internalized sense of reality and order is radically subverted. Our traditional ways of responding to situations are rendered inappropriate.

Culture shock can send tremors to the core of our very being when we immigrate. Our ego, for example, is summarily crushed by someone else's self-confident posturing. Our trust in Providence is perceived as superstitious, ineffective, non-productive fatalism. Our fragile reticence is misinterpreted as weakness of character. Our enjoyment of the present moment is misconstrued as lack of foresight and pro-activeness. Our need for company and community is seen as suffocating dependency. Respect for authority and valuing of obedience are labelled as mere subservience. An instinctive interest in other people's lives and concerns is declared invasive. Socialized to be self-sacrificing, we are overcome by the other's assertion of personal rights.

No longer of the dominant culture, immigrants become a minority among other minorities. How the dominant culture asserts itself can be seen in how the preceding paragraph, for instance, uses the passive rather than the active voice to describe what happens when we feel dominated by another culture. And worse still, we become convinced that we deserve to be dominated. We cannot even be angry.

I am sure that readers can add anecdotes about their own tragic and comic encounters of the cultural kind: how in hindsight you can laugh at them, and how at the time, you could only cry in exasperation. You may still simmer with anger. Even the luckiest among us cannot escape such turmoil. Where a gap exists between what we expect and what we get, or between what we offer and what is demanded of us, the turmoil is even greater. We are forced to live way below our own expectations. It is no surprise to find among us taxi drivers with Ph.D.s or university-educated women working as domestic helpers. Our tolerance for this gap decreases as the gap becomes permanent. Tolerance can ebb into drudging desperation as our immigrant dreams die.

Not all countries are as open to immigrants as Canada seems to be. I am not sure whether any of the minority cultures in Canada are as relatively open to one another as the dominant Anglo-Saxon-based Canadian culture is to others. I do not know French Canada. Racism and discrimination abound among fellow immigrants. Openness can be measured in terms of how a particular minority culture is ready for intermarriage, as one example, or for participation in a multi-ethnic church. Many immigrants still prefer to be among their own kind.

Even so, we experience intra-ethnic conflicts. We Filipinos have a metaphor about ourselves. We are like crabs in a boiling pot. In the heat, the stronger crabs try to crawl out; the weaker ones below unite to pull them down so that they share everyone else's lot of misery and doom. It is easier to stomach the success of other ethnic groups than it is to see fellow Filipinos succeed in a foreign land.

Besides the friendly smile we give each other as we try to ascertain a shared ethnic identity is the sideways glance that locates us on the measuring rod of success. If we score high on that scale, a host of unsaid questions is mirrored in the faces of others. "What does she do here?" or "How did she get here?" In strictly Filipino gatherings, a newcomer undertakes subtle moves to gain acceptance. Our family name immediately places us either at the bottom or the top in social ranking. We should not be so haughty that we are levelled by innuendo and aloofness. Nor should we be so self-effacing that we are completely ignored.

If we do not arouse jealousy, we become a status symbol for Filipino immigrant dreams: if only everyone else were that lucky. For example, a strong sense of identification develops and I get a lump in my throat as I watch the Filipina who has won a Tony award for her role as Miss Saigon take Eponine's role in the tenth-anniversary celebration of the musical *Les Misérables*. She is a successful actor on an essentially Caucasian stage.

By the same token, something inside me winces when I read of a Filipino suffering abroad. I can read no further; I put the book down.

But woe to us if we do something publicly outrageous that embarrasses other Filipinos. In a parish talent show, a Filipina volunteers to sing. She sings from her heart, but wanders from the tune. The other Filipino parishioners are in an uproar, demanding that she apologize for embarrassing the rest of them. Our parish priest cannot fathom such a reaction.

I often wonder how long it takes for minority immigrants to consider themselves Canadian. When asked, I still respond that I am a Filipina with Canadian citizenship. I go "home" to the Philippines, even though it no longer feels like home. From there, I return to Toronto, where home is now. I sardonically wonder how long we must live here before we want to defend Canada in the manner of the anthem's "stand on guard for thee." If an aggressor bombed Canada, would we enlist in Canada's defence, or would we pack up and go back to our country of origin? Or if Canada were to wage war on our country of origin, with whom would we side? Would we still be considered Canadian or would we be fenced out as the enemy, as Japanese-Canadians were during World War II?

As immigrants, we know all too well that we must come to terms with our predicament. We unconsciously negotiate our way towards adaptation. Some cultural areas are negotiable. We will learn English, of course; be more assertive; be more self-sufficient. There are also non-negotiables: for Filipinos, they are respect for elders, religion and family.

Cultures differ in what they prize as non-negotiables. These could be their language, their religion, their costumes, their food or their traditions. The receiving culture accommodates them to the extent that they do not constitute a major threat to its integrity. Wherever the Chinese are, there is also Chinatown. The significant Hispanic presence in the United States has made Spanish translations of English signs and notices necessary in public places.

By and large, the Philippines is the most Westernized nation in Asia. Filipinos find it easier to adjust to life in Canada than do other ethnic groups from Asia, despite the harsh winter. But we generally do not negotiate our religion and the devotions that give it life. Where Filipino immigrants abound, parishes seem to come to life.

Yet, like other immigrants, we may still silently grieve. Acceptance of our condition may involve a kind of dying. We go through periods of denial, anger, bargaining and depression, which are mitigated by our preparedness to change, no matter how inadequate we feel, and by our resilient self-possession, no matter how much it is tested.

It must also be admitted that immigrant life is not all dismal, dark and gloom. In immigrant communities we often find humour, harmless gossip, laughter, festivities, singing, dancing, parties, picnics and happy noise. Life bubbles beneath the dreariness of the everyday. In fact, immigrant cuisine, music, fashion and other aesthetic peculiarities can be much more easily adopted by the host culture than our own immigrant pain or loss or hopes or disappointments. Would that our lives as immigrants might be like the multi-ethnic food courts in our malls!

The crisis of religious faith

Immigrants' experiences of God in their native culture become inaccessible to them in the new one. What the new culture provides as vehicles for a religious experience can seem too superficial, too cerebral, too wordy, too awkward, too foreign, too cold and too distant to touch the soul. We feel empty, experiencing a void that language cannot name. We lament, more often than not, without tears and voices. Losing our emotionally satisfying sense of the holy, we also lose a sense of reality. Thrown into precarious waters, as it were, we face oppressive opaqueness that cannot hold as our life is overwhelmed by chaos. Prayers that used to give comfort become inadequate. We face an impassable abyss. God is nowhere. "My God, my God, why have you forsaken me?" (Psalm 22:1)

At the beginning, I could not land a teaching job. I checked classified ads. I sent résumés that did not elicit any response. Being unemployed and unable to teach gnawed at my self-esteem. So much of my sense of self depends on my career. Being able to teach wins me a good measure of respectability. It gives me a sense of continuity with who I was before immigration. In teaching, I confidently put my best foot forward. While everywhere else I feel like I am on shaky ground, in teaching, I stand firm and strong.

My husband reminded me that I had to go out there, introduce myself to key people, establish networks, capitalize on my Ph.D. from Louvain, and wear suits instead of colourful printed dresses. Changing my wardrobe was easy. The rest was hard. I discovered that I was quite inefficient and ineffective. Hiding behind classified ads, I disliked what I saw about myself. My providential God was not parting any Red Sea for me. What I knew in my mind did not translate into constructive action. All the while my own fears, inhibitions and anxieties paralyzed me. I felt bad, and I felt guilty about feeling bad. I cried. I prayed, "My God, my God, why have you forsaken me?" (Psalm 22:1) So much drama unfolded inside myself, while outwardly, my story was simply an attempt to find work.

I booked appointments with people. Each attempt involved thirty minutes of simply staring at the phone and writing down a nice script to read while I mustered the courage to finally call someone. I continued sending my résumés like flyers all over the place. A theologian at Georgetown University graciously granted me an audience and took me to lunch; she facilitated a part-time temporary teaching assignment for me at Georgetown. Other teaching stints eventually came my way. I followed the same method of operation in Toronto. Another kind woman working for the archdiocese agreed to meet with me and also treated me to lunch. One résumé landed on the desk of the then Dean of Students at St. Augustine's Seminary. I moved to Toronto for one course assignment at the seminary, with the hope of other prospects after I had finally become a landed immigrant.

I realize that other immigrants have had a harder time than I. Any receiving culture has an unwritten code of acceptability that allows different degrees of belonging. Other immigrants experience more difficulties because of language, because of the colour of their skin, their religious affiliation, their lack of sufficient transferable skills, or their age or health status. Refugees, who flee or are being forced out of their homeland rather than choosing to immigrate, tell of much more traumatic experiences.

Furthermore, not all immigrants implicate God in their predicament. In fact, the God question may not even arise, or may be dismissed as irrelevant. But if belief in God is an essential perspective for our lives, even implicitly, it does shape our moods and motivations, our sense of what is ultimately real and true and trustworthy. It colours our way of seeing beyond the material world. It sharpens our taste for both life and death, for both good and evil, for both self and the other. It hones our hearing for what lies beyond sound towards the ineffable and the silent. It sensitizes our touch for rosaries and crucifixes, for tactile sources of serenity. The smell of church incense and burning candles brings us to a level of quiet that is very reassuring.

Yet when unmet expectations send us reeling out of such an orbit, we fall into a yawning religious and theological black hole. We utter, sigh and cry our praying with a sense of derailment. Culture shock dislodges us so that we stumble into an unfamiliar realm of silence. Even our religious imagination fails, and this feels like falling into a bottomless pit.

Down there in that pit, we feel a need that is too deep for therapy, for counselling, for psychology, for economic-political response, or for personal support, even though all these interventions are important and can indeed help us alleviate our suffering. The upheaval caused by immigrating to another country threatens not only our economic, political and psychological survival, but also our religious and theological survival. Prayer and subsequent reflection no longer occur from places of comfort.

My theological degree and prayerful nature did not save me from this predicament. Feeling impoverished, powerless and alone, I lamented, "My God, my God, why have you forsaken me?" (Psalm 22:1) and "How could we sing the LORD's song in

42

a foreign land?" (Psalm 137:4) I did not invoke the God of the exodus, the God of many marvellous manifestations, or the God of triumphant liberation from Egypt, but the silent, hidden, absent God of exile.

As I began reading about the prophets of exile I was struck with a strong sense of recognition. They spoke to me of my situation. I heaved a deep sigh as I said to myself, "This is it!" I had been here before but lacked the name for the experience. Countless of times, I paused as I saw my soul stripped bare. Grieving, wondering where God was, starting all over again with my worst foot forward, I imploded. The biblical theology of exile made me see that, though I seemed lost in the netherworld, this netherworld existed within a larger horizon of grace.

If I now intersperse my narrative with prayers, it is because I can already place identifiable markers on the immigrant terrain. I invite you, the reader, to pause and pray. This desert will be home for quite a while. If a prayer refrain requires too much soul-searching, return to it later, when you are ready.

A Prayer Refrain

My God, my God, why have you forsaken me?
Why are you so far from helping me,
from the words of my groaning?
O my God, I cry by day, but you do not answer;
and by night, but find no rest.
(Psalm 22:1)

Allow your self to inhabit this psalm. Within this context give yourself permission to surface all attendant thoughts, sensations and emotions that rush out from your own sense of poverty, powerlessness and abandonment, while holding on to the faith that you are addressing God, lamenting to God.

"My God, my God, why have you forsaken me?" Repeat this lament slowly, again and again so that it can help you transport yourself imaginatively into the psalm. Own your poverty, powerlessness and abandonment. Locate yourself in your own abyss.

But as you do so, allow the psalm to carry you through as it praises God:

> Yet you are holy, enthroned on the praises of Israel.
> In you our ancestors trusted;
> they trusted, and you delivered them.
> To you they cried, and were saved;
> in you they trusted, and were not put to shame.
> *(Psalm 22:3–5)*

Pause here. Allow the psalm to shift your focus from your sense of abandonment to the God who beckons you to entrust yourself wholly. Stay in this prayerful space as you gently embody the intent of the psalm. It may help if you read slowly the rest of the psalm (Psalm 22:6–31).

Go back to this psalm again and again for many days. Let each phrase grip you. Let each phrase give you courage not only to face your sorrow but also, and more importantly, to entrust it to God.

If you can sing, sing a song of trust. If all you can do is hum, then hum a hymn.

Make a point of doing something concrete for someone who seems to be forsaken.

The prayerful journey towards the appropriation of the theology of exile begins with our sense of utter abandonment, the kind that impels us to pray before we decide there is no longer any point in praying. From this place of desolation we strongly identify with Psalm 22. Our own situation creates an empathy that closes the gap between the psalm and us. We break through the wall of difference to find the common ground created by compassion.

Something happens to our imagination. It opens us to the reality of God as revealed by Scripture. Imagination ceases to be a mere function of daydreaming, and becomes a function of beholding a more encompassing reality. So however fragile, wounded or defensive we feel, as we approach our God as well as our pain in prayer, we can tell ourselves to go gently. And when we do get on with our life, we do so with the grace that meets us when we pray.

In this sense, the function of any biblical text in prayer is akin to setting the stage for a theatrical performance. The setting focuses our attention. We expect to watch a dramatization of the human condition. We become so engrossed that the dramatization becomes the only thing that matters here and now. The dramatic tension can be such that we emote, we sympathize and we discover ourselves with its themes. We leave enriched or touched or totally entertained. Then we get on with life.

The analogy breaks down in the fact that prayer is not a make-believe world. Though it recreates, it hardly entertains. The biblical text that offers perspective enables us to pay attention to that which is most real about ourselves, about reality, about God. Reading Scripture is not the same as reading the news. Reading is praying. Within this perspective we go in and out of the text, as we also allow the text to go in and out of our existential condition. We embody the text, as the text articulates our soul.

The prayerful turn to Scripture

We cannot afford to live superficially. Neither can we be superficial when attempting to pray Scripture. We believe wholeheartedly that its words mediate not only a story of a believing community, but also a faith in an accessible God. Believing is at once an intellectual act, an affective commitment and an impetus for action. Believing is an assent to what is ultimately true, good and beautiful in life. Believing opens us unreservedly to the fullness of reality. Our doubts, our failure of nerve, and our attachment to what is safely familiar and pleasant may make such openness difficult but should not have the final say about our faith.

Praying as we believe is a decision to be led to such fullness. If the truth is too much that we look away, or if the good is so exacting that we balk, or if we always expect to feel good, we can trust, in prayer, that a far stronger grace will help us transcend our limits.

If you have come this far, then be prepared to step further into another dimension of prayer led by Jeremiah, Ezekiel and Second Isaiah.

Praying Scripture is a back-and-forth movement between our experience and the biblical text. We fill the lament "My God, my God, why have you forsaken me?" (Psalm 22:1) with our own pent-up feelings of rage, frustration, sorrow and isolation. And then we discover that the lament itself pushes us to acknowledge recesses of rage, frustration, sorrow and isolation that we want left in the dark, unrecognized, and therefore not felt. The lament pushes us even further to confront our own capacity to completely trust in God – it may reveal how superficial our trust has been, how brittle and how untested. The word of God gives comfort, but also makes us vulnerable. Vulnerability can sometimes be very unsettling.

We may ask, "How could we sing the LORD's song in a foreign land?" (Psalm 137:4) out of sheer despair because of our struggle with a new language, perhaps, or with new ways of doing things, or with feeling estranged and stupid. Then we discover that the question becomes a call to minister to others.

Our immigrant experience provides us with a privileged view of the biblical theology of exile: our unique experience enables us to allow the biblical theology to get under our skin. We know loss and homesickness. We know disorientation. We know the fragility of hope, but even so we hope, because the alternative is despair.

The prophetic ministry of Jeremiah, Ezekiel and Second Isaiah emerged after the Davidic kingdom was divided. The northern kingdom of Israel had vanished. Judah remained, but only for a while. When Jerusalem fell in 587 BCE, the Temple was desecrated, the king deported to Babylon with his people, the priesthood destroyed.

Biblical exile meant loss of land, temple, kingdom and priesthood. It was a dismantling of the people's frame of reference, their identity as God's chosen people. It was an experience of utter devastation, which was not only economic and political, but also, and essentially, religious. God seemed to have abandoned them into the hands of their enemies. "My God, my God, why have you forsaken me?" (Psalm 22:1) "How could we sing the LORD's song in a foreign land?" (Psalm 137:4)

Jeremiah, Ezekiel and Second Isaiah undertook the task of pastoral theology. Though the biblical text evidences layers and layers of editorial work, the original core is still discernible. The prophets spoke to the people as God had commissioned them. In the crisis of exile, they used rich imagery to prophesy the new actions of God that would help the people find their bearings. Only the imagination, fed by prophetic images, could make the exiled see God at work in their disastrous history.

Praying Jeremiah, Ezekiel and Second Isaiah can assist us in discerning the same God at work in our own stories. The prophets can articulate our longings for a homecoming in a foreign land.

When we turn to Jeremiah, Ezekiel and Second Isaiah, we do so not only because we identify with their suffering and undaunted hope, but also because they help us fathom our immigrant experience without fear. With their aid, we can plant our feet squarely on the soil of our loss. We can face our sense of dislocation and marginalization. We can trust that hope will indeed outlast our sense of despair and entrapment. We can bring our lives into the pages of Scripture.

The theological meaning that emerges from prayer is not only descriptive, but also performative. I, an immigrant, can view my predicament as exile. Not only do I intellectually see some fit between my experience and the prophets' theology, I also pray my way towards such a theology. By so doing, the theology of exile becomes my own. I name and live my fate as exile. If I were to pass on this theology to other immigrants, I would also have to invite them to pray their way to such an appropriation.

Some intellectual background about the biblical text is only one of the requirements for such a theological appropriation. As immigrants, we will take the theology of exile as our own, not because we read about it, but because in prayer, and through some feat of our imagination, we existentially locate ourselves in it.

And so let us pray.

A Gathering Prayer

Sit comfortably, and close your eyes. Invoke the Holy Spirit to help you gather your whole self before God.

Gradually make your breathing deeper and steadier while focusing your attention on the rhythmic rising and falling of your abdomen as you breathe in and breathe out. Call on the Spirit of God to ground your entire being in the glory, power and truth of the God of exile.

Acknowledge all thoughts, feelings and images that may flit through your mind and, like burning incense, let all these arise into the mystery of God's presence. If it helps, breathe them all out, while always staying mindful of the rise and fall of your abdomen as you inhale and exhale. It may also help to utter your favourite prayers so you stay centred.

Linger in this experience of yourself being gathered. Pray: "Have mercy on me, O God, according to your steadfast love." (Psalm 51:1)

Ask that you may be granted the grace to begin praying and to find in your journey the God of Jeremiah, Ezekiel and Second Isaiah. Amen.

Resolve to do something good for a fellow immigrant.

It is evident that praying our way towards a theological appropriation of Jeremiah, Ezekiel and Second Isaiah is assuming responsibility for our own pain. We decide to be responsible even when we feel helpless or trapped by our circumstances and by our inability to change as these circumstances demand.

Praying is not a substitute for living, for getting up in the morning to meet the day. Praying does not magically transpose us into the land of happy endings where all our wishes come true, where God is a great Santa Claus who ho-ho-ho's his way into granting us our heart's desire. We pray as we take seriously the complexities of our lives, because we believe that the horizon that Jeremiah, Ezekiel and Second Isaiah describe will make us see and act differently.

References

Zeev Ben-Sira. *Immigration, Stress and Adjustment*. Westport, CT: Praeger, 1997.

Walter Brueggemann. *Hopeful Imagination: Prophetic Voices in Exile*. Philadelphia: Fortress Press, 1986.

Matthew Frye Jacobson. *Special Sorrows: The Diasporic Imagination of Irish, Polish, and Jewish Immigrants in the United States*. Cambridge, MA: Harvard University Press, 1995.

R.G. Rumbaut. "The Agony of Exile: A Study of the Migration and Adaptation of Indochinese Refugee Adults and Children," in *Refugee Children: Theory, Research and Services*, F.L. Ahearn and J.L. Athey, eds. Baltimore: Johns Hopkins University Press, 1991.

Daniel L. Smith. *The Religion of the Landless: The Social Context of the Babylonian Exile*. Bloomington: Meyer-Stone Books, 1989.

Paul Tabori. *The Anatomy of Exile: A Semantic and Historical Study*. London: Harrap, 1972.

Charles Zwingmann and Maria Pfister-Ammende. *Uprooting and After*. New York: Heidelberg, 1973.

Jeremiah Grieves with Us

"My joy is gone, grief is upon me, my heart is sick. Hark…." (Jeremiah 8:18–19) We lift this passage out of its original context in order to find an entry point into Jeremiah's world. This entry point is where we hurt the most. An immigrant's first prayer is often the most difficult because it is the most painful. As we adjust to the demands of immigrant life, we have neither the time nor the courage to face this pain. We move from day to day, grateful for routine activities or chores; the night finds us too tired to do anything but sleep. The drudgery of the day-to-day becomes a means of avoiding this pain.

And of course, there is the bliss of diversions. There are movies to watch, video games to play, the Internet to surf, friends to see, parties or picnics to attend, the malls in which to shop or window-shop, tourist spots to visit and photograph, campsites and resorts at which to vacation (it is mostly third-, fourth- or fifth-generation Canadians who own cottages).

The joylessness, the grief, the sickness of heart remain, nevertheless, like a dull ache. After a time we push the pain out of our consciousness; to be reminded of it generates violent resistance and defensiveness in us. It is amazing how seemingly

51

reasonable objections to the construct of the immigrant experience as exile actually mask a fear of facing our own difficulties. Thus, we have to tread slowly and softly in this prayerful journey. We cannot be accidental tourists of our own soul, nor can we be haughty conquistadors of our own pain.

"My joy is gone, grief is upon me, my heart is sick. Hark…." (Jeremiah 8:18–19) Scholarship informs us that the book of Jeremiah is the product of a long history of editorial work, but Jeremiah's lament remains audible throughout. Called to be a prophet, and faithful to that ministry for forty years, he speaks out against the nation's idolatrous ways, only to find that people bitterly oppose and persecute him. He suffers a crisis of faith, which he poignantly articulates in his "confessions," scattered throughout chapters 11 to 20 of the book. When the nation falls to Babylon, Jeremiah grieves over its upheaval and loss, and dies a tragic figure.

Grieving as praying

Entering into Jeremiah's grief, as we also enter our own, is a graced event because Jeremiah places himself within a deep theological understanding. He is a grieving prophet who remains faithful to God and to his prophetic calling. He remains faithful despite the people's refusal to heed him and despite God's refusal to sugar-coat the warnings of impending doom.

Furthermore, Jeremiah experiences no vindication, even when his prophecies come true, because he sees Jerusalem devastated. Biblical exile, then, entails guilt and judgment, but also, and most importantly, it includes God's abiding faithfulness.

Jeremiah offers us the language of grief. Though immigrant suffering may not involve guilt or outright unfaithfulness to God, it can identify in other ways the experience of Jeremiah. He becomes the vehicle by which our most private grief can find its voice. In turning to Jeremiah in prayer, we may learn to embrace our own kind of exilic state.

"My joy is gone, grief is upon me, my heart is sick. Hark…." (Jeremiah 8:18–19) Taking Jeremiah's lamentation so that we, as immigrants, can face our own grief means that we pray it. Allowing Jeremiah to utter the first prayer, we allow ourselves to make his words concrete with our own particular loss of joy, our own particular grief, our own particular sickness of heart. And with him we say "Hark," addressing the same God who called him to be a prophet of exile for the exiled.

Addressing God thus, praying "Hark, God, please listen" presupposes a whole understanding of reality that many people no longer hold. For many, "God" is a name given to some amorphous being who is only invoked in emergencies, a *deus ex machina,* a "god out of a machine," a "god installed artificially to unravel a complicated plot."[3] This is God as a filler of gaps, a number for a missing equation, someone a cosmonaut thinks he will see in outer space. Seeing no one, the cosmonaut happily concludes that his atheism has been validated. This god is construed either as a being among other beings, or simply as the sigh of the oppressed whose wishful thinking has no compelling claim to truth. This is the god of family traditions, invited to certain feasts that merit an expensive visit to a professional photographer, but completely ignored the rest of the time.

Praying "Hark, God, please listen" implies a faith in God as an all-abiding personal and gracious presence. And if the God we know from childhood discourages intimate praying, then perhaps allowing Jeremiah to utter our prayer also allows him to reveal God to us.

We will now explore the *lectio divina,* an ancient practice of praying Scripture. Literally translated as "divine reading," it flows from reading a text to uncovering its spiritual significance to sustaining our total presence before an Other who has chosen to be present to us in word and, therefore, in ways accessible to the human mind. The *lectio divina* also supports the intent of dialogue in which God and the one who prays can address each other in communion. In communion, all words recede to the background once they have been spoken; what remains is a presence of one to an Other.

The *lectio divina* is a journey in which the mind that understands opens to the heart that emotes and feels. Ultimately, the response is felt at the ground of our being, where we face the gut issues of faith, trust and hope, where we make the leap. The *lectio divina* presupposes and sustains a ritual of gathering. We gather our mind, our heart, our body, our soul – all the aspects of our immigrant experience – and place them in the presence of God. This gathering rite invites us to relax our stiff upper lip, to unlock suppressed anxieties and anger, to offer our sagging energies and will to survive, because we are in the presence of God. We gather ourselves from our many dispersions and sense of brokenness so that, at least in this particular space and time of prayer, we are truly ourselves. The space of prayer becomes a space of freedom as God gathers us into God's own self.

The *lectio* part of the *lectio divina* is already prayerful reading. It requires attentiveness both to the text and to what it evokes in us. *Lectio* is listening to what cries out to be articulated within us and to what God wills to communicate in and to us. The more we are totally present to the text that provides the scaffolding for our prayer, the more self-revelation will ensue. God becomes more real to us as well. Because we are praying, our self-revelation is positioned before God, who is as present there as we are to ourselves and to the text.

Meditatio begins our conversation with the text. We inhabit the text. We become the characters therein. We realize our unworthiness before God's utter goodness. We respond to the call to conversion.

Meditatio leads to *oratio*, when we articulate our selves unto the Lord, speaking spontaneously, lamenting, crying, complaining, raging, seeking mercy, demanding justice and invoking grace until, like a vessel emptied, our souls are laid bare before God. We become our own prayer.

Contemplatio begins. In silence, beyond what can be put into words, we simply are. When we think we have arrived at the end of our praying, we find ourselves on a threshold where we simply are before this all-encompassing reality we call God.

Inherent to the *lectio divina* is the movement towards depth or height or breadth. A text is a particular point of departure that opens up to a total personal engagement. The text transposes us towards communion with God. The *lectio divina* is not a one-dimensional process of reading and reflection that leaves untouched much of who and what we are. Something happens to us when we attune ourselves to the drumbeat of true prayer.

There is a point within the *lectio divina* when words surrender to the ineffably true, the irresistibly good and the delightfully beautiful: the Holy One. Within the biblical understanding, the Holy One is God, whose gaze is continually cast upon the whole of creation. Intimacy with God means sharing such a loving gaze. One begins to love better and to incarnate that love in one's own tiny reality.

The *lectio divina* lifts our consciousness from its focus on the day-to-day only to return it to the same day-to-day but already imbued with ultimate significance by God as revealed in Scripture. The *lectio divina* is a way of approaching Scripture that requires our willingness to be fully carried into this close encounter with God. We have to choose to be moved step by step in the process. Though logical and natural, the movement from *lectio* to *meditatio* to *oratio* and to *contemplatio* does not happen on its own accord without our consent. We can refuse to open our understanding. We can refuse to relinquish our safe objectivity. We can resist the attractiveness of contemplation.

The *lectio divina* cannot be hurried. Requiring not only our total participation, but also our patience, it is a spiritual discipline that will eventually become a way of being.

The *lectio divina* bridges the distance between Jeremiah's era and ours, a distance created by time, place, culture and the way we think we know what is real. His words become our prayer words.

A *Lectio Divina* on Jeremiah 8:18–19

Lectio

Read and reread the following text until it gives full voice to your own sense of displacement: "My joy is gone, grief is upon me, my heart is sick. Hark…." (Jeremiah 8:18–19)

Meditatio

Words may not be adequate to articulate our grief. We may not even wish to grope for the words. Praying with Jeremiah enables us to be open to God and to our own situation. We courageously position ourselves thus, because this is the framework that gives meaning to all the negativities that attend our crossing over to another culture.

Our negativities have so many names: conflict, threat, loss, resistance, dismantling, combat, disappointment, forlornness, hostility, crisis, danger, pain, dis-ease, disequilibrium, hurt, turmoil, psychic paralysis. Despite all these burdens, in Jeremiah and in prayer, we find a safe place in which to grieve.

Our grief as immigrants can be as heartbreaking as Jeremiah's, the changes we face as overwhelming, the alienation as threatening, the hurt as paralyzing. Jeremiah teaches that unless we acknowledge and weep over the hurt, we will never find a homecoming. When the hurt and the grieving are allowed their say, we also confront the fact that, beyond the psychological, practical, linguistic, cultural, social, economic and political up-heavals that attend our crossing over to another country, there is the other loss, that of our sense of being anchored in God. God seems to be absent, and we grieve.

Handing over grief to prayer becomes an act of faith that enables us to accept our displacement. Even if our grief is not assuaged – indeed, praying with Jeremiah may heighten it – we will know that our very particular grief has found a spiritual home. Jeremiah has been there before us.

Our second act of faith as immigrants who have discovered (or been discovered by) the language of grief in Jeremiah is to trust in the good news that God is right there at the heart of grieving. God grieves with us. We can submit to grief because by so doing, we submit ourselves to the inscrutable, suffering mercy of God.

The third act of faith is the silent expectation that newness can come forth from the tomb of inescapable, inevitable grief.

Handing our selves over to Jeremiah's grief, we summon the courage to face our own grief without being weighed down by it or being tempted to wallow in it. Jeremiah has carved out a clearing in the dark forest of human anguish where, he pro-claims in trust, the God of healing and salvation can be in-voked, and where healing and salvation can indeed come.

Thus, we can take comfort in God's word:

But as for you, have no fear, my servant Jacob, says the LORD,
and do not be dismayed, O Israel;
for I am going to save you from far away,
and your offspring from the land of their captivity.
Jacob shall return and have quiet and ease,
and no one shall make him afraid. For I am with you,
says the LORD, to save you....

(Jeremiah 30:10–11a)

I have loved you with an everlasting love;
therefore I have continued my faithfulness to you.
Again I will build you, and you shall be built....
(Jeremiah 31: 3b–4a)

I will put my law within them, and I will write it on their
hearts; and I will be their God, and they shall be my people.
(Jeremiah 31:33b)

I will make an everlasting covenant with them, never to draw
back from doing good to them; and I will put the fear of me
in their hearts, so that they may not turn from me. I will
rejoice in doing good to them, and I will plant them in this
land in faithfulness, with all my heart and all my soul.
(Jeremiah 32:40–41)

Call to me and I will answer you, and will tell you great and
hidden things that you have not known.... I am going to
bring [you] recovery and healing; I will heal [you] and reveal
to [you] abundance of prosperity and security.
(Jeremiah 33:3–6)

But as for you, have no fear, my servant Jacob,
and do not be dismayed, O Israel;
for I am going to save you from far away,
and your offspring from the land of their captivity.
(Jeremiah 46:27a)

Praying our grief, in the space of trust that Jeremiah provides, ultimately means surrendering ourselves to God. Jeremiah's text may strike us cognitively at first, but if we remain
open, it will then prod us to uncover feelings that move us to
tears. Furthermore, if we so allow, the text can express the fullness of our inner experience. As we become wholly present to
the text, we also become wholly present to God.

Oratio

Give yourself freedom to express everything to God. Prayer is not words you have memorized; prayer addresses your entire self to God.

Contemplatio

After you pour out your thoughts and feelings, rest on one word that sums up your prayer (e.g., trust, surrender, help, why, lament). Assume that word wholly. Don't *think* the word, *be* the word; don't *feel* the word, *be* the word. Be.

Linger in this prayerful posture for a while. You will discover that you are no longer hurried and harried. Some serenity envelops you while keeping you attentive and awake. Strength, courage, wholeness may filter through your whole self. Even a sense of closure will tell you wordlessly that here, at this moment, you can end the *lectio divina* with an Amen.

Do something concrete for immigrants in your midst.

God's grieving

Jeremiah prays "Hark," at times not knowing to whom he should address himself. He speaks harsh words to God's people, warning them to "circumcise [themselves] to the LORD, remove the foreskin of [their] hearts" (Jeremiah 4:1-4). In fact, right after Jeremiah's call to be a prophet (Jeremiah 1:4-13), we hear God's litany of lamentations over the people's infidelity:

> What wrong did your ancestors find in me
> that they went far from me…?
> *(Jeremiah 2:5a)*

Has a nation changed its gods,
even though they are no gods?
But my people have changed their glory
for something that does not profit.
(Jeremiah 2:11)

Yet I planted you as a choice vine,
from the purest stock.
How then did you turn degenerate
and become a wild vine?
(Jeremiah 2:21)

Why do you complain against me?
You have all rebelled against me....
(Jeremiah 2:29)

The lamentations go on and on, and yet God still calls, even begs:
Return, faithless Israel...
I will not look on you in anger,
for I am merciful....
I will not be angry forever.
(Jeremiah 3:12b)

Return, O faithless children,
I will heal your faithlessness.
(Jeremiah 3:22)

If you return, O Israel, says the LORD,
if you return to me,
if you remove your abominations from my presence,
and do not waver, and if you swear, "As the LORD lives!"
in truth, in justice, and in uprightness,
then nations shall be blessed by him,
and by him they shall boast.
(Jeremiah 4:1–2)

God says, "Hark," but the people do not listen. We often presume that God does not listen to our prayers. Jeremiah, in fact, tells us otherwise. It is we who have forgotten how to listen, our forgetfulness aggravated not only by our distance from Jeremiah's world, but also by our presumption that we are too enlightened and too modern to be biblical.

The failure to listen is an insidious thing. At times we do not know if anyone will really listen to us. It takes too long for us to form the words so that others will understand. Sometimes we do not want to listen to our own pain or grief or sickness of heart. Life becomes a series of daily chores that prevents us from facing our overwhelming emotions. Jeremiah says, "Hark," telling us, as immigrants, also to pay attention to what we find difficult to acknowledge.

The people reject Jeremiah as they reject God's word. Called to take a stand against Jerusalem's unfaithfulness, Jeremiah has to pronounce judgment and make such pronouncements his own. Jeremiah has become part of God's message, however unbearable the tension – "My anguish, my anguish! I writhe in pain! Oh, the walls of my heart! My heart is beating wildly; I cannot keep silent; for I hear the sound of the trumpet, the alarm of war." (Jeremiah 4:19)

Unrelenting, God laments and foretells disaster. Unrelenting, Jeremiah speaks on God's behalf. Unrelenting, God's people remain obstinate. Caught between a rock and a hard place, Jeremiah mourns, "My joy is gone, grief is upon me, my heart is sick. Hark…." (Jeremiah 8:18–19)

Interspersed with Jeremiah's "Thus says the LORD," the text sustains the heightened pathos behind God's lamentation and judgment of the people's refusal to keep the terms of the covenant. Harsh words describe the people's unfaithfulness. It is defilement, abomination, transgression, apostasy, whoring, perversion, foolishness, stupidity, falsehood, adultery, betrayal, slander, deceit, iniquity, oppression, idolatry, wickedness, treachery.

Caught in this tension, Jeremiah finds himself totally alone, interceding for a people who, though they have rejected him and God, have no one else to whom they can turn:

> Have you completely rejected Judah?
> Does your heart loathe Zion?
> Why have you struck us down
> so that there is no healing for us?
> We look for peace, but find no good;
> for a time of healing, but there is terror instead.
> We acknowledge our wickedness, O LORD,
> the iniquity of our ancestors,
> for we have sinned against you.
> Do not spurn us, for your name's sake;
> do not dishonour your glorious throne;
> remember and do not break your covenant with us.
> Can any idols of the nations bring rain?
> Or can the heavens give showers?
> Is it not you, O LORD our God?
> We set our hope on you,
> for it is you who do all this.
> *(Jeremiah 14:19–22)*

Burdened with God's word, which the people reject, as well as with the people's wretched situation, Jeremiah becomes the righteous one who suffers. He remains obedient to God, and continues to be the sole intercessor for God's people. Jeremiah prays "Hark" as he accepts the people's affliction as his own. Without him, God's people would lose their own voice and their chance to pray.

> Hear me, O LORD, and I shall be healed;
> save me, and I shall be saved,
> for you are my praise.
> See how they say to me,
> "Where is the word of the LORD?
> Let it come!"

But I have not run away from being a shepherd in your
service,
nor have I desired the fatal day.
You know what came from my lips;
it was before your face.
Do not become a terror to me;
you are my refuge in the day of disaster;
Let my persecutors be ashamed,
but do not let me be shamed;
let them be dismayed,
but do not let me be dismayed;
bring on them the day of disaster;
destroy them with double destruction.
(Jeremiah 17:14–18)

Jeremiah assumes this burden knowing that the community opposes and disbelieves his prophetic words. He cannot keep silent, because he must speak God's word and because Judah must lament its dejection. As he speaks, Jeremiah speaks both God's word and Judah's. As he is eventually silenced, he assumes the silence of Judah and the silence of God.

"My joy is gone, grief is upon me, my heart is sick. Hark…." (Jeremiah 8:18–19) We turn to Jeremiah because he knows exile. He knows bereavement. He knows loneliness. He knows lamentation. He knows abandonment. But he also knows that this exilic state is the place to call on God.

Grieving as tending towards God

Grief in Scripture is not a private sorrow. It is laid at the entrance to God's sanctuary. Even in its extreme form of wishing one's enemies ill — "Happy shall they be who take your little ones and dash them against the rock!" (Psalm 137:9) — grieving situates us within a relationship. Even raging grief is prayer, is entrusting ourselves to God. Even when lost, we cry out to be found.

Such a difficult form of prayer initiates us into a deeper and more vital relationship with God. Grieving that is also praying personalizes a faith that for a time might have been only a habitual and external observance of religion. It is this more personal movement towards God that grants meaning to grief. Otherwise, by itself, grief can become a step towards psychological, emotional and spiritual disaster. Grief for grief's sake can become a kind of narcissism that draws the sufferer, as well as anyone who wants to help, into a downward spin towards oppressive self-absorption. Some people endlessly talk about their tragedies for the sheer negative pleasure and for the control they exert on the one who cares enough to listen.

Praying our grief frees us from this temptation, because although we grieve, we also face God, who wants to heal. We have to grant ourselves permission to be healed.

To enter the world of Jeremiah is to know God and to learn to speak to God the way Jeremiah did:

> You will be in the right O LORD,
>   when I lay charges against you;
>   but let me put my case to you.
> Why does the way of the guilty prosper?
> Why do all who are treacherous thrive?
> You plant them, and they take root;
>   they grow and bring forth fruit;
>   you are near in their mouths
>   yet far from their hearts.
> *(Jeremiah 12:1–2)*

Woe is me, my mother, that you ever bore me, a man of strife and contention to the whole land! I have not lent, nor have I borrowed, yet all of them curse me.

(Jeremiah 15:10)

I did not sit in the company of merrymakers,
nor did I rejoice;
under the weight of your hand I sat alone,
for you had filled me with indignation.
Why is my pain unceasing,
my wound incurable,
refusing to be healed?
Truly, you are to me like a deceitful brook,
like waters that fall.
(Jeremiah 15:17–18)

Heal me, O LORD, and I shall be healed;
save me, and I shall be saved;
or you are my praise.
(Jeremiah 17:14)

Give heed to me, O LORD,
and listen to what my adversaries say!
Is evil a recompense for good?
(Jeremiah 18:19–20a)

O LORD, you have enticed me,
and I was enticed;
you have overpowered me,
and you have prevailed.
I have become a laughingstock all day long;
everyone mocks me.
(Jeremiah 20:7)

Why did I come forth from the womb
to see toil and sorrow,
and spend my days in shame?
(Jeremiah 20:18)

Jeremiah's confessions reveal a man audacious enough to question God. If we learn to pray like Jeremiah, nothing in our situation as immigrants need be judged too banal, uncouth or blasphemous to be prayer.

Many people give up the faith of their childhood once failure or sorrow or frustrations set in. They give up on God when their petitions are not granted. There cannot be a God when nature and human history mercilessly take their own course, and no superhuman being intervenes in their favour, they believe.

In Scripture, failure or sorrow or frustration is a new beginning; it opens the door to a more mature way of praying. Childish faith gives way to intimate knowledge of God. Just when we are at the point of giving up, we start to move forward.

> Then I will gather the remnant of my flock out of all the lands where I have driven them, and I will bring them back to their fold, and they shall be fruitful and multiply. I will raise up shepherds over them who will shepherd them, and they shall not fear any longer, or be dismayed, nor shall any be missing, says the LORD. (Jeremiah 23:3–4)

> The days are surely coming, says the LORD, when I will raise up for David a righteous Branch, and he shall reign as king and deal wisely, and shall execute justice and righteousness in the land. In his days Judah will be saved and Israel will live in safety. And this is the name by which he will be called, "The LORD is our righteousness." (Jeremiah 23:5–6)

The God of Jeremiah takes no pleasure in suffering, but neither does God want us to pretend that there is no suffering. God desires that we face the truth of our situation. The God of Jeremiah cannot countenance the prophets of false hopes and expectations who paint rosy pictures that hide a painful reality.

The God of Jeremiah wants to save, but we must know from what we are to be saved.

> Thus says the LORD of hosts: Do not listen to the words of the prophets who prophesy to you; they are deluding you. They speak visions of their own minds, not from the mouth of the LORD. They keep saying to those who despise the word of the LORD, "It shall be well with you"; and to all who stubbornly follow their own stubborn hearts, they say, "No calamity shall come upon you." (Jeremiah 23:16–17)

The exilic state, the nadir of our life, is the last place we want to be. Our coping mechanisms can so easily become attempts to hide from our own sorrow. We turn our backs on it, and wonder why living is so exhausting. We ignore the howling demons within and instead fight battles over petty transgressions, such as being cut off in traffic. If we continue to avoid our existential pain, we cease to feel it. Yet it can linger, catching us off guard when we look at ourselves in the mirror and see our pain staring back.

The distance we create between us and our state of exile also puts distance between us and the God of Jeremiah. Knowing this God is not a matter of tinkering with the divine name. Cerebral manoeuvres only empty the God of Jeremiah of vitality. A God who is overly conceptualized and objectified cannot be the God who can save us.

> Am I a God near by, says the LORD, and not a God far off? Who can hide in secret places so that I cannot see them? says the LORD. Do I not fill the heaven and earth? says the LORD.... Is not my word like fire, says the LORD, and like a hammer that breaks a rock in pieces? (Jeremiah 23: 23–24, 29)

> Like these good figs, so I will regard as good the exiles from Judah, whom I have sent away from this place to

the land of the Chaldeans. I will set my eyes upon them for good, and I will bring them back to this land. I will build them up, and not tear them down; I will plant them, and not pluck them up. I will give them a heart to know that I am the LORD; and they shall be my people and I will be their God, for they shall return to me with their whole heart. (Jeremiah 24:4–7)

Jeremiah positions us where it hurts the most because only truth sets us free to be before God. Jeremiah's complaints are not a perverse fixation on disaster but a prophetic task, wrestling us out of the cocoon of denial. The aggression Jeremiah suffers from his own people reveals how denial can turn us against God and, ultimately, against ourselves. The priest Pashhur persecutes Jeremiah (Jeremiah 20:1–3). The priests and prophets in the Temple threaten to put him to death (Jeremiah 26:7–11). The prophet Hananiah opposes him (Jeremiah 28:1–17). Officials arrest and imprison him (Jeremiah 37:11–16). Army commanders force him to sojourn in Egypt, where he dies a heartbroken man (Jeremiah 43:1–13).

Our resistance to praying the immigrant experience as exile increases when such prayer begins with Jeremiah.

Jeremiah not only prepares God's people for impending exile, he also helps them accept their situation as a way to conversion. Only God can bring about a change of heart. Exile is the yoke around their necks (Jeremiah 27:1–22). Exile means building houses and living in them, planting gardens and eating what they produce, taking wives and having sons and daughters, seeking the welfare of the city where they have been sent (Jeremiah 29:1–23). Exile is buying the field at Anathoth (Jeremiah 32:1–25).[4] Exile is dying in peace in Babylon (Jeremiah 34:1–7). Exile means remaining in Babylon as a remnant of Judah (Jeremiah 42:1–22). Life goes on, even in exile.

Only when it is transformed into prayer can grief stop short of despair. Exile is the place for praying, "My joy is gone, grief is upon me, my heart is sick. Hark…." (Jeremiah 8:18-19) Bringing our own pain into the pages of Jeremiah's book, we can dare to pray: "But you, O LORD, know me; You see me and test me – my heart is with you." (Jeremiah 12:3)

We can lament: "Why is my pain unceasing, my wound incurable, refusing to be healed?" (Jeremiah 15:18) Or we can implore: "Heal me, O LORD, and I shall be healed; save me, and I shall be saved; for you are my praise." (Jeremiah 17:14) We can call: "Give heed to me, O LORD." (Jeremiah 18:19)

The Book of Lamentations and some Psalms articulate our heartache

Beyond the Book of Jeremiah, we encounter other scriptural texts that we can appropriate as a language for our grieving. The Book of Lamentations consists of five poems whose author (or authors) was obviously familiar with the harsh events of exile. "How lonely sits the city that once was full of people! How like a widow she has become, she that was great among the nations! She that was a princess among the provinces has become a vassal." (Lamentations 1:1) To lament is not only to cry out, but to "cry out to the heavens." It is a kind of grief that splashes onto the canvas of eternity. To lament before God is to lay claim to God's fidelity while fully acknowledging one's unworthiness. Not to lay claim to God's fidelity means irrevocable self-damnation. Despair will run its ultimate course.

In chapter 3 of Lamentations, we find the poet sustaining the tension between despair and hope. God's mercy is inexhaustible. "The thought of my affliction and my homelessness is wormwood and gall! My soul continually thinks of it and is bowed down within me. But this I call to mind and therefore I have hope: The steadfast love of the LORD never ceases, his mercies never come to an end; they are new every morning; great is your faithfulness." (Lamentations 3:19–23)

When we seek to be informed by Scripture, we find ourselves cradled by a fundamental act of faith, so that even giving
vent to torrents of grief becomes better than building a dam to
contain it. The poet of Lamentations undertakes the same pastoral ministry as Jeremiah's: to help us pray our way through
our own sense of exile in the hope of a homecoming. "Restore
us to yourself, O LORD, that we may be restored…." (Lamentations 5:21a)

A number of psalms can give voice to our own particular
homesickness. Psalm 137 can serve as an immigrant's anthem.
In Psalm 44, we find the psalmist raging against God's seeming
powerlessness to avert the tragedy that has befallen God's people. The psalmist complains that God has rejected them. God
has to be roused from sleep, from inaction. The psalmist pro-
tests against the people's fate, no matter how much they have
earned it through their unfaithfulness. If I do not scream at
you, God, I will turn into a pillar of salt. "Rouse yourself! Why
do you sleep, O LORD? Awake, do not cast us off forever! Why
do you hide your face? Why do you forget our affliction and
oppression?" (Psalm 44:23–24) As immigrants, we can also take
this as our own cry. When placed in the flow of the *lectio divina*,
such a cry leads us to the still, wordless moment of simply
being present to God.

The specific circumstances surrounding my own joylessness or grief or sickness of heart seem unimportant to recount
now. I tend to have very dramatic reactions to my rather undramatic life. But I can say that I bear them with all the courage I can muster. Such courage finds strength in the grace that
descends on me not only because I pray, but also because I live
from day to day, doing the things that I must do. I am grateful
for these chores and responsibilities – buying groceries, cook-
ing, taking care of my family, preparing my lectures, teaching –
because all these provide me with structure. Too much preoccupation with grief can be paralyzing. My contemplative mo-

ments occur not only in prayer but also in the rhythm of cutting up vegetables for the family dinner or in pushing my daughter's stroller when she was little.

Participating in the Sunday liturgy also situates my life within a larger story. Singing my faith has always been uplifting. I know the cathartic effect of belting out the hymns at Mass, really meaning them, and allowing the melody to express the interior cry for help that otherwise would not have been released. Outside of Mass, when my mind fills up with useless thoughts, my heart brims over with negative feelings or my guts tighten into knots, I hum a hymn and find relief.

Music seems able to reach deep into the inner chaos of my soul. Music, with its melody, its tonality, its rhythm, its inherent dynamic, provides focus, perspective and a sense of order and rightness. It brushes away useless thoughts. It soothes the heart. It grounds my soul in something so captivating that I am moved to hope, even before my mind realizes that I am hoping. I continue with my head above water. Life simply and relentlessly moves on.

Seeing a spiritual director has also helped me. Jesuits who are schooled in the discipline of discernment have made sure that I do not leave any stone unturned. After listening quietly to my weepy incoherence, the first Jesuit to help me declared that perhaps Jesus was handing me over to the Holy Spirit. He did not offer a detailed explanation of this comment, but it opened my imagination. I became able to frame my experiences in a meaningful way without wishing away the negative parts. I understood, without being able to explain in conceptual terms, what this meant. It took me a long time to unpack this pithy assessment. When I lose perspective, I always return to this frame, and something, some irresistible grace, always buoys me up so I can bear my suffering, instead of having my suffering needlessly weigh me down.

Psalm 74 teaches that our faith in God may lead us to an awful place where brute forces of history simply take their course and God seems mute, unmoved and powerless. For many people, the loss of faith is the logical consequence. Paradoxically, by being invited to pray, we can use this as the starting place to make bold assertions about God's care and power. Biblical faith is never forged when we are well-funded and well-fed. Biblical faith finds firm resolve in confessing God's eternal providence even if we are overrun by disaster. "Do not let the downtrodden be put to shame; let the poor and needy praise your name. Rise up, O God, plead your cause; remember how the impious scoff at you all day long. Do not forget the clamour of your foes, the uproar of your adversaries that goes up continually." (Psalm 74:21–23)

Anyone who helps immigrants adjust to their new country (for example, through teaching a new language, job-training, house-hunting, counselling) knows that if they allow themselves to be vulnerable, the immigrant's pain will rub off on them. A theological understanding of the immigrant experience will offer a way of situating that vulnerability in God. Before even talking about Jeremiah's grief to an immigrant, that person needs to acknowledge silently that that grief is there: expressed, masked or even denied.

Ministering to immigrants must be suffused with this graced capacity simply to be present. This ministry of "being with" builds a sense of community. To minister is to bring people together. Acts of hospitality – in a church basement, in a school gym, in a home – will convey to immigrants that there are people to turn to, a place to go, someone to call. Acts of hospitality give the assurance that somewhere in this strange, cold country is a place of refuge. Immigrants, too, can be hospitable. They may find it easier to share their food, music and dance than their pain and anxiety.

Once a level of comfort or trust is established, a conversation can begin or end with a simple, "Will you allow me to pray with you?" In a Christian environment, it is appropriate to pick a psalm, the Lamentations, or texts from Jeremiah and proclaim the redeeming word. No homily is necessary. Neither are comments such as: "I understand how hard it is for you to be here." The text speaks for itself and for the unspoken experience.

Biblical language presumes a covenant with God. Though Psalm 79, for instance, is a lament, it also rests on the conviction that God is faithful to God's people. God must act justly while showing mercy. "Help us, O God of our salvation, for the glory of your name; deliver us, and forgive our sins, for your name's sake." (Psalm 79:9)

When we bring our immigrant experience to prayer, we express not only our deepest anguish, but also our faith that the God we address will hear our lamentation. This is the God who declares: "I have loved you with an everlasting love; therefore I have continued my faithfulness to you." (Jeremiah 31:3b) So the author of Psalm 102 can lament in hope. Hope is hope in God. God is deserving of all praise. Praising God within one's loss is a declaration that no devastation is ever final; there shall be restoration. "For the LORD will build up Zion; he will appear in his glory. He will regard the prayer of the destitute, and will not despise their prayer." (Psalm 102:16–17)

Cries of distress sunder the heavens, and God responds. We lament knowing that God hears; we lament because we have experienced deliverance; we lament because we know that God is there. To lament is to entrust ourselves to God's blessing.

A Prayer Refrain

Give yourself time to make this psalm of trust your own:

Into your hand I commit my spirit; you have redeemed me,
O LORD, faithful God
(Psalm 31:5).

If you are seated as you are praying, imagine your whole weight resting not only on the seat, but also on God's unfailing trustworthiness. Repeat the prayer slowly and rhythmically.

Repeat the prayer again and again while allowing your abdominal area to relax. Unknot all knotted feelings as you find your breathing deepening without being forced.

Continue repeating the prayer, while unburdening your heart. Include everyone whom you care for in this prayerful process of unburdening. Allow all tensions to rise up and leave you through your neck and your head. Imagine all cares and woes rising up out of you to the love of God that, though imperceptible, surrounds you and holds you.

Repeat this prayer until you feel that you are really entrusting yourself and everyone in your care to God. Linger in that space of serenity and sense of being gathered in love. You may wish to end this prayer refrain with a favourite prayer or simply with an Amen.

Do something concrete for a fellow immigrant.

A coda for the reader

We have just gone through a first round of praying Scripture. The particular prayer events within the text guide our attention from superficial reading to a sense that we are before

God. The prayer events confront us with our own deeper reality. Then they transpose this reality as prayer, in which we are wholly before God, and God, as revealed by Jeremiah, is also there before us.

Several activities might help you explore further. You might start a prayer journal to record your own narrative. You may wish to see a spiritual director. Or you could start a prayer group so that you will not feel so alone.

You might also be moved to read Jeremiah on your own. Using the pedagogy of the *lectio divina*, you slice into the seeming incomprehensibility of the text, if only with the basic understanding that you are praying and that the text expresses God's and your own personal reality.

This approach to Scripture is very Trinitarian. Scripture is the first "person" of this trinity. You, the praying one, are the second. The meaning that unfolds in the back-and-forth movement between the biblical text and your experience is the third. Each angle in this triangle is distinct, but the total experience is one. If we puzzle over the mystery of the Trinity, this experience provides a window through which to behold and contemplate it. There is always a third "person" in any given situation. Between two friends is friendship. Between teacher and learner is the challenge to learn. Between an artist and the art is beauty. Between lover and beloved is love. The Trinity is not a puzzle to be solved, but a mystery to enter. We understand mystery the way we understand love or beauty or the immensity of creation or another person. But such an understanding does not close the issue. Rather, it ushers us into something that comprehends us instead.

This approach to Scripture is of itself an exercise of resonance and dissonance. The world of Scripture is far removed from our reality; unless we approach it in prayer, it will remain closed to us. Sometimes, when we approach it prayerfully but lack any intelligent background to the text, we are sidetracked into considering irrelevant details or, worse, into using Scripture to support our self-righteous narrow-mindedness. We need to be reminded that Scripture has not only enlightened, but has also darkened souls into bigotry and hatred.

Some people hesitate to embrace Jeremiah's message because it belongs to the Old Testament. Christians who were taught to regard the Old Testament simply as a preparation for the New may not see that Old Testament themes are as relevant to our Christian life as those found in the New Testament.

The first time I introduced a parish to the possibility of reading the immigrant experience as exile, a woman approached me and admitted that she found the state of exile no longer applicable to Christians because of Jesus' resurrection from the dead. For her, Christ's resurrection had essentially rendered Old Testament themes obsolete. I wonder if we can grasp the full significance of the resurrection if we do not see it in unbroken relationship to the cross. I wonder if we can have a comprehensive understanding of the cross without knowing what it means to be in exile and to yearn desperately for a homecoming.

The pedagogy of the *lectio divina* prepares us not only for the revelatory nature of Scripture but also for a process of praying towards contemplation. Before the birth of modern biblical scholarship in the nineteenth century, Christians were able to draw on Scripture for their personal and ecclesial life because they prayed, meditated on and contemplated it. Practical, moral, theological, even mystical wisdom flourished before the onset of modern scholarship.

Yet the findings of biblical scholarship do not render praying Scripture unnecessary. Knowing about Scripture cannot substitute for experiencing it as mediating God. Scholarship should still be at the service of prayer. Biblical scholarship that is divorced from prayer makes Scripture powerless to transform our lives. Alone, scholarship goes on in its periscopic objectivity, always above the water. Alone, prayer submerges into the murky ocean, undiscerning and ignorant about the difference between faith that sees and superstition that blinds. Together, prayer and scholarship help us bridge the gap between the faith communities behind the original texts and us. The scriptural text stands on the experiences of real people, with real religious struggles, whose frail humanity and wavering faith we also can claim as our heritage. This text is not a string of words hanging in emptiness. It reveals their world and opens us to ours, to God, and to fundamental questions.

Allow this personal theology to mediate between Jeremiah and your immigrant experience, and allow Jeremiah, Ezekiel and Second Isaiah to name your condition as exile. My joy is gone, grief is upon me, my heart is sick. Hark…. (Jeremiah 8:18–19)

References

Walter Brueggemann. *To Pluck Up, and to Tear Down: A Commentary on the Book of Jeremiah 1–25*. Grand Rapids, MI: Eerdmans, 1988.

Guy P. Couturier, C.S.C. "Jeremiah," *The New Jerome Biblical Commentary*, ed. Raymond E. Brown, S.S. et al. Englewood Cliffs, NJ: Prentice Hall, 1968, 1990, 265–297.

Ralph W. Klein. *Israel in Exile: A Theological Interpretation*. Overtures to Biblical Theology. Philadelphia: Fortress Press, 1979.

Timothy Polk. *The Prophetic Persona: Jeremiah and the Language of the Self*. Journal for the Study of the Old Testament, Supplement Series 32. Sheffield, England: JSOT Press, 1984.

Claus Westermann. *Praise and Lament in the Psalms*. Keith R. Crim and Richard N. Soulen, trans. Atlanta: Knox Press, 1965, 1981.

Ezekiel Reveals the Glory of God

"O dry bones…you shall live." (Ezekiel 37:4–6) As Jeremiah provokes the release of grief, he also leads us into prayer as an ever-deepening journey. Jeremiah hands us over to Ezekiel. And if you think this is going to be an easier ride, don't hold your breath!

To behold the glory of God

Ezekiel's inaugural vision makes apparent that this ever-deepening journey of prayer is uncanny, provoking uneasiness because one is in the presence of the uncomfortably strange, the unfamiliar, the mysterious, the supernatural.[5] Ezekiel contemplates a stormy wind with a great cloud surrounded by brightness and fire flashing forth continually. In the middle of the fire, something gleams like amber, and contains four living creatures, each with a human form, each with four faces: the face of a human being, the face of a lion, the face of an ox, and the face of an eagle. Each has four wings, two of which touch each other, while the other two cover their bodies. In the middle of them is what looks like burning coals of fire, like torches moving to and fro, and lightning issues from the fire. Over their heads a dome shines like crystal. Above the dome there is a throne like sapphire in appearance, and seated above is what seems like a human form. Ezekiel sees something that looks like fire, with splendour all around like a bow in a cloud on a rainy day. This is the appearance of the likeness of the glory of God. (Ezekiel 1:4–28) Falling on his face, Ezekiel hears a voice speaking: "Mortal, I am sending you to the people of Israel…and you shall say to them, 'Thus says the Lord God.'" (Ezekiel 2:3–4)

Ezekiel beholds the glory of God – bright, flashing, gleaming, burning, lightning, shining, fire. And he is sent forth as God's prophet speaking "words of lamentation and mourning and woe" (Ezekiel 2:10c), words that he must eat and fill his stomach with, tasting sweet as honey in his mouth. (Ezekiel 3:3) He will speak to the exiled by the river Chebar. (Ezekiel 3:12–15) He is to be the sentinel for God's people, to speak and to remain silent as God wills, calling the wicked to repent, and the righteous not to sin. (Ezekiel 3:16–27)

More than this, Ezekiel must enact God's judgments on God's people in ways as bizarre as his inaugural vision. He has to take a brick, against which he is supposed to put siegeworks, a siege wall, a ramp, camps, battering rams and an iron wall. (Ezekiel 4:1–3) He has to lie on his left side to bear the punishment of Israel. (Ezekiel 4:4–5) Then he has to turn on his right side to bear the punishment of Judah (Ezekiel 4:6–8), drinking only water and eating bread of wheat and barley, beans and lentils, millet and spelt, baked on cow dung. (Ezekiel 4:9–15) He must cut his hair and his beard, one-third of which he shall burn, one-third of which he shall strike with the sword, and one-third he shall scatter to the wind. (Ezekiel 5:1–4)

Ezekiel displays a classic religious response of awe, wonder, adoration and reverence before a manifestation of the divine.

Likewise, he lives out this response in complete obedience to God's bidding. As in Jeremiah, God's self-validating revelation is the source of Ezekiel's prophetic vocation. God grants Ezekiel the purity of sight to behold, the silence to listen, and the heart to embody God's glory for God's exiled people. When Ezekiel announces his "Thus says the Lord" to the exiled, he does so as the prophet of God's glory.

Ezekiel beholds the glory of God and speaks on its behalf, but he does more than this: he embodies it. Because he does, he stands outside the boundaries of the ordinary or normal. Biblical scholars tell us that Ezekiel is not a study in pathology. Nor is his ecstatic experience of God to be taken as the most accurate portrayal of the divine that we can finally commit to memory. We are not meant to immortalize it in art and liturgy. Neither are we to establish this vision as the goal that our spiritual disciplines should replicate. Rather, in Ezekiel we face God's self-assertion of absoluteness that defies human circumvention. God breaks down and through all human constructs for purposes that exceed our imaginings.

The glory of God is Ezekiel's answer to our grieving prayer – glory that is judgment, glory that wills to possess our whole being, though our being cannot contain it. It is glory that seems at odds with our scheme of things. Thus, Ezekiel's answer seems to be no answer at all, or at least, not the answer we expect. At the outset, Ezekiel makes us realize that before we can be consoled by "O dry bones…you shall live" (Ezekiel 37:4–6), we have to reckon with God, whose glory is bright, flashing, gleaming, burning, lightning, shining, fire, and before which Ezekiel falls on his face in obeisance.

Ezekiel declares a God who is vastly different from our homespun theologizing. This is so not only due to the unusual nature of his vision, or to the even more unusual symbolic acts that he performs. Ezekiel declares a personal God who takes the initiative to gratuitously bestow divine glory, not because we have earned it, but because God abounds in it. God's glory comes close to us because of God's own ebullient generosity, which overflows our grasp. God reveals God's own glory not as a token of divine appreciation for our "burnt offerings and elaborate propitiations." (Psalm 51:15–17) This limitless bounty, this bright, flashing, gleaming, burning glory, this lightning, this shining fire wills to give of itself wholly to us, as a free offer desiring free acceptance. "O dry bones…you shall live." (Ezekiel 37:4–6)

Yet we do not realize this. For one thing, the glory of God is not an everyday occurrence. Even if it is experiential, it is usually mediated by our ordinary life. God does not make our concrete existence irrelevant or unimportant by upstaging it, as it were, with divine glory. Something like Ezekiel's experience may break through, but this is more the exception than the rule. The glory of God does not obliterate Ezekiel or swallow us up.

We hold in faith that one day, beyond this earthly life, we will see God face to face. For now we take seriously how our life unfolds, because there is no other route by which we can gain some intimations of God, no matter how difficult they may be to discern.

Second, not having Ezekiel's purity of sight, silence and heart, we do not consider that we are in the presence of this glory. Our life can be all-consuming and therefore closed off to transcendent reality. Or, although we may be open to a transcendent dimension, we still are far removed from acknowledging that experiencing something like God's glory is possible.

Third, a biblical world view does not always engender such openness. The story of God's people is a story of falling away and turning to God and falling away again.

Fourth, although we turn to God in our grief, we may see only our own struggle. We may hear only our own lamentation. We may be prejudiced by our own wishes about how our life should turn out, especially if we pray. We may presume a good return on our investment.

Praying can become self-serving, a straining towards some desired result: a recompense for our losses, a lessening of our disorientation, an expedient passage through in-betweenness, and a homecoming on our own terms. God may be our last recourse, but we want God to serve our ends, to be subservient to our praying.

What seeps into us is a kind of self-righteousness that makes us conclude that, because we are not like those others who do not even call on God, we should have the advantage, we should be at the right hand of the Lord as he sits on his throne of glory.

Our praying becomes our security deposit, our guarantee. A certain frantic busyness invades us. We string mass offerings, novenas and votive candles. We think that the longer we sit in prayer, reciting the fifteen mysteries of the rosary each day, the more chance we have of being heard. The more people we ask to pray for us, the more saints we invoke, the louder will our prayer be in the halls of God's kingdom. The more retreats or seminars on prayer and meditation or bible study sessions or experiments in yoga or Zen or incursions into the world of the enneagram and chakras or explorations into cutting edge theology, the easier it is to hold God answerable to us, and for us to emerge as the one in control.

Praying becomes wrestling with God in order to alter the course of our fate. When things don't get better, or even get worse, we reach our limit and conclude that there may not be any point to praying at all. We experience the futility of prayer.

Jeremiah may have taught us to truly pray, but Ezekiel becomes for us like a crucible that purifies the way we pray. Grief may have opened prayer's door, but we must walk through it. We may expect only consolation and the granting of our heart's desire, but instead we meet God. Prayer becomes a person-to-person encounter, requiring our total presence, not merely the memorized formulas or devotional practices that carry our petitions. Prayer requires that, in addition to bringing our requests, we come into the presence of the Giver of all good things. It is jarring when we realize that we are more interested in what we can get from praying than we are in God.

God comes to us in all glory, but due to our religious consumerism, we are unprepared for what this entails. No one warns us beforehand what prayer will be like. Rather than seeing God's glory, we see what it illuminates. God's glory exacts brutal honesty. Caught off guard, we see our raw humanity exposed. We may come to know who we really are for the first time: "O dry bones…." (Ezekiel 37:4–6)

The glory of God is judgment. In the wake of Ezekiel, we learn that the truth God reveals about us is excruciatingly painful. We can resist this. We can refuse its cutting judgment. But it is the only truth that saves. No wonder Ezekiel, like Jeremiah before him, is full of warnings of destruction, desolation and ruin. (Ezekiel 6:1–9:11) The glory of God destroys, makes desolate and ruins our bastions of untruth. The glory of God unmasks us.

Praying becomes self-discovery. We have deeper and darker regions of our being, a seemingly bottomless inner region, a hole in our soul from whence the instinctive, even irrational, roots of our thoughts, feelings, motivations and desires unexpectedly arise. The grieving that vents as flowing tears actually harbours fear, anxiety, anger, rage, terror and panic that are still unexpressed. Here, where things are not neat and tidy, we are under the unflinching scrutiny of the God of Ezekiel. We bear the harsh realization that we cannot face even ourselves squarely. Who can stand the glory of God without being burned?

The estrangement we experience as immigrants is bad enough. This new estrangement is worse. Our heart is heavily laden. We are sinners. Any attempt to justify ourselves only reveals our smugness. Admitting our guilt can unwittingly plunge us into a quagmire of self-loathing. Humility suffocates under the weight of our humiliation. Obsessive breast-beating renders our prayer for forgiveness mute. We cannot even be at home in our own skin. We are waylaid deep inside ourselves and our sense of loss and disorientation increases.

We find that we no longer have the God we used to know or the self we used to prize. Prayer ceases to be consoling. We cannot not pray, but neither can we leap out of our own skin. Trapped in this conflict that is far more painful than the clash of cultures, we aggravate our predicament. We are drawn further into a region of in-betweenness.

Like the valley of dry bones, this place is gloomy, murky, cold, heavy, burdensome and sad. We try our best to rise above the unwelcome feelings it evokes, but to no avail. We can no longer patch the hole in our soul.

As memories collide with expectations, as hurts fester, the part of us that seems wiser and more resilient struggles with the part that wants to give up. When we try to avoid this gaping abyss, for fear of falling, other emotions take control of us. Rage explodes over minor provocations. We take offence when none is intended; when a store clerk or bank teller ignores us or bypasses us for another customer, we ask ourselves, "Would they have done the same thing if I were white?"

Praying becomes arduous. The only liberating choice is to entrust our whole self to this judgment that promises that we shall live. We slowly learn to allow God's glory to make us bare. This bright, flashing, gleaming, burning lightning, this shining fire, uncovers everything.

Our contemplative tradition calls this soul-rending process "purgation." In Ezekiel, it is a lifetime-and-beyond process of becoming holy, because God is holy. Purgation does not take place because we have to be made worthy before God will care for us. It takes place because God cares for us and desires to remove, layer by layer, whatever hinders intimacy.

On the existential level, this often feels like we are being unduly punished. We may be tempted to flee. We check to see if grief's door is still ajar so we can scamper away. Maybe it is better to see a counsellor or a therapist who can psychologize everything away, we think. There must be a Twelve Step program for immigrants who pray. If I just read about and practise the seven secrets of successful people, I will be okay. If I think positively, look on the bright side, grin and bear it, I'll get by. Maybe more meditation exercises will help. Maybe dabbling in Buddhism is better: at least Buddhism suggests that suffering is optional.

While academic theology may make my faith intelligent, I risk being quite informed, but not transformed, by it. Feeling out of sync with myself and with life in general, I return to my valley of dry bones. There I repeat my Hail Marys. For a long time, I am stuck in the sorrowful mysteries of the rosary. As my finger moves from bead to bead, unnamed feelings clash with unwieldy thoughts, and my religious instincts collide with my academically critical mind. Meditation books and breathing exercises only re-enforces my self-preoccupation. Asleep or awake I feel burdened.

When I dare to confront the hole in my soul, my instinct to pray falters. I find release in teaching, since what I teach contains lessons I need to learn for myself.

The dark place is confusing, disconcerting, threatening and terrifying. Except for grace, we cannot remain mired here long. Except for grace, we cannot even imagine that all this takes place in the light of God's glory. Except for grace, we cannot shift our gaze slowly from our own selves to the God of Ezekiel, who is there all the while and whose penetrating light shines upon us so that we see.

Ezekiel falls on his face to reverence God's glory. How do we do the same when all we see is darkness? How do we pray when God's presence feels like a drawn-out absence? How do we stop this frenzied self-preoccupation that keeps on plucking at our own pain? Where do we find the courage to pass through this crucible? It is a kind of dying. "O dry bones…you shall live." (Ezekiel 37:4–6)

My culturally formed religious instinct and my Louvain-educated theological mind fall into this abyss. The normal commerce of life goes on while spiritually I flounder. Knowing that I am before God but unable to account for how I know, I flutter my wings in panic. Where is the escape hatch? On second thought, *can* one escape?

> Holy darkness, blessed night,
> Heaven's answer, hidden from our sight.
> As we await You, O God of silence,
> We embrace Your holy night.[6]

This liturgical song is inspired by a poem by John of the Cross, a sixteenth-century Spanish mystic. Its lyricism and melodiousness have been a calming balm for my soul. Singing along allows me to move from an obsessive, anxious focus on myself to God, who seems so far away but who, Ezekiel says, is close at hand as transcendent glory. I repeat it again and again because this is the only prayer that gives me courage. Jeremiah has handed me over to Ezekiel. And I sing, "Holy darkness…."

The uncanny is the distance between God and us. It marks the radical difference between Creator and creature. When we collapse this difference into a metaphysical or theological blob, we risk ascribing to creation the quality of the divine. Alternatively, we risk ascribing to the divine the totality of all reality, thereby making us mere passing shadows, drops that disappear without a trace into the immense ocean.

When we allow the distance, we honour it. Yet that reverential response issues from us only as we release all pent-up doubts, unbelief, guilt and misgivings that God is a figment of our imagination, a mere residue of an uninformed religious upbringing. Our notions of God cannot stand the test of our life, which takes on its own uncaring course. We risk becoming agnostics or atheists as we teeter beyond the edge of our comfortable religion. We are haunted by a nameless malaise, a disquieting sense of futility and desperation, a frantic search for healing, a hold on some relief for our existential anxiety, a rush to overcome loneliness without knowing the way towards intimacy.

It may be difficult to sustain our faith from within this chasm that only God can bridge, but this is what makes contemplation possible. Even in human interpersonal terms, we need to stand back from the other in order to see. If we get too close, we can smother or be smothered. If we are too close, our vision becomes skewed.

God reveals God's own self here in this space. This God, the God of Jeremiah, Ezekiel and Second Isaiah, the God we come to know as immigrants, the God beyond culture, is not a mere projection of our mind. The biblical testimony insists on the distinctiveness of this self-revealing God. The prophetic tradition is even more adamant in its assertion of God's uniqueness against the people's deep-seated tendencies to be idolatrous. This God is irreducible to anything human, but at the same time is so intimately close, participating in the travails of human history. This is God whose glory is bright, flashing, gleaming, burning, lightning, shining, fire. Like Ezekiel we fall on our faces in obeisance.

A Prayer Refrain

Pause to absorb the preceding paragraph. Let it lead you to the mode and mood of prayer. Light a candle, if you wish. If it helps, close your eyes. As you make your breathing deep and steady, invoke the Holy Spirit's presence.

Acknowledge all thoughts, concerns and feelings that surface in your consciousness. Rather than pursuing each thought or feeling or concern, try to hold it in your heart, bearing it as an offering to God.

To sustain this openness to God, do as the psalm instructs:

> Ascribe to the LORD, O heavenly beings,
> ascribe to the LORD glory and strength.
> Ascribe to the LORD glory of his name;
> worship the LORD in holy splendour.
> *(Psalm 29:1–2)*

Allow the whole of your being to pray it. Focus on your breathing. Let your breathing "ascribe to the LORD glory of his name." Focus on your abdomen. Let it "ascribe to the LORD glory of his name." Focus on your chest. "Let it ascribe to the LORD glory of his name." Focus on your throat. "Let it ascribe to the LORD glory of his name." Move on to your neck. "Let it ascribe to the LORD glory of his name." Move to your forehead. "Let it ascribe to the LORD glory of his name." Move to the crown of your head. "Let it ascribe to the LORD glory of his name."

As you embody the invocation of this psalm, imagine your whole being giving glory to God. Rest a while in the silence and freedom this prayer refrain allows.

Ascribe to the LORD, O heavenly beings,
ascribe to the LORD glory and strength.
Ascribe to the LORD glory of his name;
worship the LORD in holy splendour.
(Psalm 29:1–2)

If an enlarged sense of peace descends upon you, linger in that grace for a few minutes. Be thankful. Be resolute to be more attentive and responsible for your situation. It is always good to say "Amen."

Do good for someone to celebrate as well as to reverence the glory of God.

Something radical happens to us in this prayer: we lose ourselves as we give God glory. Granted the light to acknowledge who we really are, we now acknowledge, in this same light, the One who deserves all glory. This liberation from self-preoccupation is one of the most freeing experiences we can have; it is also the embrace of the uncanny. We inhabit our valley of dry bones with only the prayer that reverences God in all glory. "Then you shall know that I am the LORD." (Ezekiel 6:7).

Knowing that "I am the LORD" is the essence of contemplation. Here we bring our senses to rest in what is beyond their grasp. Here the mind abides in what thought cannot hold captive. Here the heart finds repose beyond its desiring. Here our whole self finds the assurance to simply be, without self-satisfaction or self-justification or self-damnation or self-negation. Our entire being assumes reverential openness to that which forever surrounds us and that which we can never encompass. We can be disciplined to achieve a certain level of openness, but there is no spiritual technology to make grace reveal itself according to our expectations.

Outside the purview of reverential openness, ascribing to God all the glory can have deadly effects on our psyche. It can create an image of a narcissistically monstrous being who over-whelms us with an impossible demand. The freedom of self-forgetfulness turns into suppression of the self. Praying becomes a chore. Contemplation becomes straining for something that drains us of all joy.

Truly contemplating God's glory does not suspend our senses or our thoughts or our desires or our selfhood. Without putting us under some hypnotic spell or into some fictional world, contemplating God's glory heightens our awareness of the ultimate dimensions of all reality. Ezekiel's response tells us that such an experience is wholly engaging and salvific.

Even non-religious contemplative moments are wholly en-gaging and salvific. Just imagine the effect that the sight of a sleeping baby or a rainbow has on us. Part of the effect of contemplation, though, is that we try to freeze the moment and hold on to it. We seek to imprison it within the limits of our imagination. We hope it will fill the expanse of our incom-pleteness.

To know God as the Holy One

The book of Ezekiel is an attempt to put into human terms God's will to be known as the utterly Holy One. God cannot be domesticated, circumscribed, coded or mastered. Ezekiel speaks, in another vision, of four wheels that gleam like beryl (a gem) beside each of the cherubim. They are wheels within wheels within wheels. When they move, they move in any of the four directions without veering. Their rims, their spokes, their wings are full of eyes all around. The cherubim have four faces: the first is that of a cherub; the second, a human being; the third, a lion; and the fourth, an eagle. The cherubim lift their wings and rise up. (Ezekiel 10:9–17) "Then the glory of the LORD went out from the threshold of the house and stopped above the cherubim. The cherubim lifted up their wings and rose up from the earth as they went out with the wheels beside them." (Ezekiel 10:19–20) God departs from the Temple to be with the exiled in Babylon.

Ezekiel declares a God who is absolutely free, absolutely holy. Though so close, God is also ungraspable. Though self-revealing, God also conceals. Though captured in Word, God is also intractable Silence. Though immanent in creation, God is always unfathomable, transcendent mystery. Giving this God all glory is a leap of faith, a leap into that mystery.

God's holiness pervades the whole of reality. It is when we acknowledge this, albeit in the darkness of faith, that we will begin to come home. "I will gather you from the peoples, and assemble you out of the countries where you have been scattered." (Ezekiel 11:17b)

I will give them one heart, and put a new spirit within them;
I will remove the heart of stone from their flesh and give
them a heart of flesh, so that they may follow my statutes,
and keep my ordinances and obey them. Then they shall be
my people, and I will be their God.
(Ezekiel 11:19–20)

But I the LORD will speak the word that I speak,
and it will be fulfilled.
(Ezekiel 12:25)

Yet I will remember my covenant with you
in the days of your youth, and I will
establish with you an everlasting covenant.
(Ezekiel 16:60)

All the trees of the field shall know that I am the LORD.
I bring low the high tree, I make high the low tree;
I dry up the green tree and make the dry tree flourish.
I the LORD have spoken; I will accomplish it.
(Ezekiel 17:24)

For I have no pleasure in the death of anyone,
says the LORD God. Turn, then, and live.
(Ezekiel 18:32)

At certain moments in prayer, we can maintain this utter self-disposal unto the Lord. But once we are thrust back into our everyday lives, we lose perspective again. There are certain circumstances we want changed. What good is it if only we are changed? What good is it if we ascribe to God all the glory? What about our sense of loss or disorientation? What about our longing for a homecoming? "My God, my God, why have you forsaken me? (Psalm 22:1) And "How could we sing the LORD's song in a foreign land?" (Psalm 137:4)

The story of God's people in the Bible – their blindness, disobedience, stubbornness and idolatry – is our story, too. Idolatry is essentially a loss of perspective. We do not linger long enough to simply be before God who IS. We do not want the freedom this grants.

So God rages for God's own holiness. A cursory reading of Ezekiel gives the impression that God is selfish, punitive, angry and mean. (It is amazing how we tend to outgrow most of our childish notions except those that have to do with God.) Scripture gropes for language to express how God rages, the way the Song of Solomon describes raging love: "strong as death, passion fierce as the grave. Its flashes are flashes of fire, a raging flame. Many waters cannot quench love, neither can floods drown it." (Song of Solomon 8:6–7a)

God vindicates God's holiness – awesome, sublime, majestic, cosmic, tremendous, salvific. "But I acted for the sake of my name, that it should not be profaned in the sight of the nations among whom they lived, in whose sight I made myself known to them in bringing them out of the land of Egypt." (Ezekiel 20:9)

Holiness makes love inviolable, innocence disarming, truth compelling. It is that inner quality of goodness that makes us want to be good. It is that which draws from us awe, wonder, adoration and worship.

Ezekiel creates a scenario filled with vehement images. God's self-vindication is wrath, anger, destruction, scattering, dispersion, horror, fury, indignation, which explode against the people's abominations, defilements, rebellion, rejection, profanation and idolatry.

We do not realize that these images are ways of communicating the idea that we cannot transgress the holiness of God with impunity, that they put into words the fatality of human sinfulness; we have a distorted picture of a vengeful and wrathful being. We are filled with neurotic feelings of guilt and foreboding. To liberate ourselves from this, we take the other extreme – playing with words, convincing our sophisticated selves that we simply need cognitive therapy. To cushion our comfortable lives, we envisage God as being like a well-manicured lawn, lacking rough edges.

A vibrant life of faith contains a lot more dramatic tension than we dare imagine, and is not always pleasant. Discordant experiences, like the immigrant experience and its deepening journey in prayer, prove that. When we cover up the discordance, God will be like a sword drawn from its sheath to cut through our denials (Ezekiel 21:1–32), like fire in a smelter that removes the dross from the silver. (Ezekiel 22:22)

Like Jeremiah, Ezekiel knows exile. An ecstatic prophet, he sees visions of God's grandeur and proceeds to declare that Israel must be a holy nation. His extraordinary passion reveals how hard it is to break through the walls of sin. Even as we turn towards God, we are asked to surrender to the call that we be as God IS. Contemplation brings about transformation. The loving intimacy that God desires for us happens. Our contemplative tradition calls this the unitive moment, the moment in which God the Lover and we, the beloved, are held in love.

For thus says the LORD God:
I myself will search for my sheep,
and will seek them out.
(Ezekiel 34:11)

But you, O mountains of Israel,
shall shoot out your branches,
and yield your fruit to my people Israel;
for they shall soon come home....
Then you shall know that I am the LORD.
(Ezekiel 36:8, 11b)

Thus says the LORD God: It is not for your sake, O house of
Israel, that I am about to act, but for the sake of my holy
name.... I will sanctify my great name...and the nations shall
know that I am the LORD...when through you I display my
holiness before their eyes.
(Ezekiel 36:22–23)

O dry bones... you shall live.
(Ezekiel 37:4–6)

I will save them from all the apostasies into which they have
fallen, and will cleanse them. Then they shall be my people,
and I will be their God.
(Ezekiel 37:23b)

My dwelling place shall be with them; and I will be their
God, and they shall be my people. Then the nations shall
know that I the LORD sanctify Israel, when my sanctuary is
among them forevermore.
(Ezekiel 37:27–28)

So I will display my greatness and my holiness and make
myself known in the eyes of many nations. Then they shall
know that I am the LORD.
(Ezekiel 38:23)

My holy name I will make known among my people Israel;
and I will not let my holy name be profaned any more;
and the nations shall know that I am the LORD,
the Holy One in Israel.
(Ezekiel 39:7)

The consequence of this loving surrender is the receiving of "a new heart and a new spirit." (Ezekiel 11:19–20) The divine initiative occasions the appropriate human response. Everything rests ultimately on the mysterious nature of God, who acts so it might be known that "I am the LORD," and so that we find our being only in God.

A *Lectio Divina* on Ezekiel 37:4–14

Lectio

Read and reread the entire passage and then focus on this short line until it seeps through your entire being: "O dry bones…you shall live." (Ezekiel 37:4–6)

Meditatio

No image captures exile more profoundly than that of the valley of dry bones. The weight of death oppresses. Unable even to sigh, we cannot raise ourselves up from the heavy sadness of the scene. Grey and wan, these bones spell the apparent finality of the exilic state. All effort to resist such a fate has been exhausted. There are no more tears to be shed. We are at a point where new birth is impossible, where death becomes appealing, and where the message "you shall live" (Ezekiel 37:6) is difficult to receive. We can grow accustomed to being dry bones.

How can we live when nothing is right within? Our experience is at odds with our expectations of God. As our hurts

96

settle to a familiar dull ache, we are overcome by a pervasive sense of utter loneliness. No one will turn everything into a happy ending for us. Grief is still grief. Homesickness is still homesickness. Inadequacies remain inadequacies. There is no one to blame, no one to forgive.

We have silenced our questions about how to reconcile belief in a good God with the reality of suffering. We have accepted the hard facts: there is no place to hide, no clever plan to even the score. Not even the God we think we know provides relief. We have become used to the agony of alienation and disorientation.

We have stopped seeking an adequate language for our situation. In the valley of dry bones, language fails. Here is only silence. We are past the need for words. We have resigned ourselves to our immigrant life. We will always have these knitted brows, deep lines around our mouths, tight jaws, hunched shoulders, dragging feet. Would that we could just stop breathing. Would that we could just slump in defeat. Would that the longing stopped, the regrets ceased, the "what if's," the "if only's," the "why did I ever's" halted. Would that we could just go back home without the stigma of failure. Would that we could start afresh where no one knows us. Would that fairy tales came true. Would that there was gold at the end of the rainbow.

We listlessly keep on living because stopping now, just even pausing to see ourselves, dry bones that we are, might deplete us even more. It no longer helps to grieve. It no longer helps to ask why.

But it is here, Ezekiel tells us, that we are utterly exposed to the Holy One who desires only to come close and bridge the gulf that separates us. Here we can receive what God longs to give, reduced as we are to a wordless prayer, a mute plea for salvation. "I will cause breath to enter you, and you shall live. I will lay sinews on you, and will cause flesh to come upon you, and cover you with skin, and put breath in you, and you shall live; and you shall know that I am the LORD." (Ezekiel 37:5–6)

The vision of the valley of dry bones promises restoration for the exiled then and for us now. Ezekiel's insistence on God's holiness is his pastoral response to the exilic predicament. It is judgment, but it is also a sure promise of a homecoming.

Outside the context of prayer, the uncompromising nature of God's holiness seems brutal, even sinister. Preached as a platitude, offered as an off-the-cuff remark to someone dealing with a tragic situation, laid down as a prescription to shortchange the long process of moral discernment, the holiness of God, like its correlate, God's will, turns into a lethal poison to the soul. No one wants anything to do with this kind of God.

Revealed more starkly at disjunctive moments in our lives, the holiness of God grounds and surrounds the whole of created reality. When we cry, "My God, my God, why have you forsaken me?" (Psalm 22:1), we may feel like we are at a dead end, but we are called to surrender ourselves to God.

God's holiness becomes the sole reason for such surrender. Jeremiah helps us pray in our grief. Ezekiel helps us surrender to all that this entails, and thus learn fidelity to a life of prayer and its power to transform.

Ezekiel's words are tough, but he also submits to silence. Ezekiel knows the silence of God as God departs from the Temple. There must be silence because the devastation of God's people is unspeakable. There must be silence for us as well because, in the valley of dry bones, what is there left to say?

Our silence, our loss for words, can flow into the silence of God. Our silence, our loss for words, can flow into God – bright, flashing, gleaming, burning, lightning, shining, fire.

Paradoxically, the sense of freedom that this act of faith creates comes with the graced realization that we are limited and fragile; God is so much greater and more gracious than we can imagine. In God's own good time, for the sake of God's holy name, God will allow us to find our home in God's transcendence.

Like Ezekiel, we become sentinels of God's epiphany. We can accept the darkness without being deadened by it, because we see it now through the perspective of God. In the meantime, we will live on. There is no escape anywhere. Day-to-day obligations are a welcome respite. We will celebrate and have fun. Note the many ethnic restaurants and ethnic-based festivities where immigrants abound. We will still have moments of blissful abandonment in the ordinary pleasures of human life.

When we appropriate Ezekiel's passion for the holiness of God, we confront issues of guilt and moral responsibility — perhaps not because we are immigrants but because we are sinners. Ezekiel's radical theocentricity is a guard against the human tendency to be presumptuous. Ezekiel keeps us from our fixations on comfortable, familiar notions of God, as if God could be reduced to our terms and conditions. We are prevented from considering God functionally. Ezekiel calls us to religious maturity that should be construed not only cognitively (i.e., in our ability to rationally account for what and why we believe), but also affectively (i.e., in demonstrations of deep and abiding trust), and practically (i.e., in actions and "works of faith").

Our prayer life will have to pass through this crucible. Our prayer life will be thrust into the awesome unmanageability of God, in which we are denuded of our pet images and notions of who and what God is and should be. We will let go of these notions even if we instinctively want to hold on.

This explains why prayer, both personal and communal, is central to our appropriation of the theology of exile. As in the time of exile, when liturgy was the only link that those banished to Babylon had to the heritage they had lost, our experience of upheaval, loss, grief, disorientation and hope can find its anchor in prayer. Even if prayer ceases to be a comfortable refuge, it becomes the threshold where we humbly entrust ourselves to the One who says, "I am the LORD." "O dry bones…you shall live." (Ezekiel 37:4–6)

Oratio

Give yourself freedom to express everything to God.

Contemplatio

After you have poured yourself out to God, rest on one word that encapsulates your prayer (e.g., trust, surrender, hope, confident waiting, humility, being present, "help!", "why?", lament). Assume that word wholly. Don't *think* the word, *be* the word; don't *feel* the word, *be* the word. Be.

If an enlarged sense of peace descends upon you, linger in that grace for a few minutes. Be thankful. Be resolute to be more attentive and responsible for your situation. It is always good to say "Amen."

Do something enlivening for someone who might be quietly suffering through the "valley of dry bones."

Prayer that passes through the crucible leads us to the very ground of our being, including but not limited to our minds and our hearts. Teresa of Avila teaches that there at the ground of our being, we are wholly in God; there no sin, no evil, no violation can ever penetrate us. We do not lose consciousness. Rather, we become more conscious of the richer dimensions of our interior life. We are not transported out of our bodies. Rather, we are as fully present to ourselves as we can be.

Technically called the anagogical moment in prayer, the uncanny transforms what has caved within into a palpable space of grace and blessing. There we feel whole. There we become self-possessed because of a gratuitous and irresistible knowledge that we are held in love, held by God.

The gift of communion with God is at the same time a communion with others that leads to compassion for the plight of other people. Communion with all the saints ceases to be a mere article of the Christian creed. It becomes real. In fact, the whole creed becomes real, revealing its riches to those who pray.

Such an understanding generates more presence to day-to-day life. I will not have trusted my own journey of prayer if it has not made me more attentive to the mundane and the ordinary. It is so easy to hide inside ourselves. The human psyche can become a world unto itself. We can literally sulk inside ourselves and cease to live. And I sing, "Holy darkness…."

It is at the anagogical moment, at that moment when all human constructs waver in their limitation, that the ineffably real purifies and integrates them into itself. The space between "My God, my God, why have you forsaken me?" (Psalm 22:1) and "Into your hand I commit my spirit; you have redeemed me, O LORD, faithful God" (Psalm 31:5) is not a vacuum. There, we make the decision to trust nevertheless, but also to respond to a summons to do what is right, and to be where truth, goodness and beauty lead, to seek a "new heart and a new spirit." There, we find a moment of lucidity wherein we choose life or death, self-absorption or redemption.

All fear, even irrational, visceral or psychological fear, is overcome if we call on the LORD. But we should not see God as magic that we invoke at whim, for that is blasphemous. Nor should our faith be mindless, for God is Word made flesh, willing to be understood in human categories. Neither should our faith be imprisoned by our concepts, because all mental categories break down before the experience of the Holy One.

The dry bones shall live because of God's holiness. When everything fails, when the disjunctions caused by our immigrant experience bring us to this holy night, we can entrust ourselves wholly to God. This prayerful posture during this night is the hardest to sustain. So I sing, "Holy darkness…."

I light candles, I hold on to my rosary. I move on with the day. I spend quiet moments sitting in a church where I can watch the votive candles flicker. I go to Mass. I do my daily chores. I teach. I live. Concreteness, materiality, bodiliness and sentience are like markers I hammer onto my spiritual geography to remind me always that the seeming absence of God is God's transcendent way of being present to me.

To be thus transformed by God's holiness

To pray in the wake of the prophets of exile transforms our imagination so that it becomes biblical. This does not mean that we become adept at quoting biblical passages by heart or at lacing our conversation with biblical quotations. It means, rather, that biblical images so shape our imagination that we see how our present reality is permeated by so much more meaning, so many more possibilities, more risks, more nuance, more dimensions. As these images penetrate our being, we begin to see that our life itself is a *lectio divina*. We begin to see that biblical themes become a way of discerning how God is at work in our present history. Immigrant experience is exile.

The biblical is very earthy, corporeal and human. What is palpable to the senses points to the transcendent. As it points, it remains palpable. It does not disappear into oblivion as it manifests the divine. In the experience of grace, we do not leave behind what is material and earthy, to glory happily in the spiritual. The spiritual suffuses our materiality with the presence of God. The material becomes a sacrament of the presence of God.

The biblical, therefore, retains the tension between materiality and transcendent reality. Within this tension, we experience God through what we see, touch, hear, taste and smell. At the same time, God remains distinct from our sensible experiences, and because God is, God grants the ultimate meaning to all our embodied experiences.

Ezekiel's faithful ministering to the glory and holiness of God involves detailed specifications about the Temple, measuring cubits in length, cubits in breadth, cubits in thickness. (Ezekiel 40:1–42:20) Nowhere do we find anything more concrete, material, bodily and sensate than the Temple. It circumscribes the presence of the Holy One in the midst of the people, with walls, gateways, steps, recesses, thresholds, vestibules, barriers, courts, windows, shutters, chambers, pavements, stairways, tables, pegs, naves, sidewalls, inner rooms, stories, platforms, panels, doorposts, altars, canopies, galleries, passages, exits and entrances.

Ezekiel's specifications configure space – at once personal, geographical and material – to contain God's presence. Space becomes holy space. "And the glory of the LORD filled the temple." (Ezekiel 43:5b)

Within this holy place, God ordains rituals of purification, atonement, cleansing and consecration, offerings and festivals at certain days and within specific timelines, while assigning roles, functions and lifestyle to the priestly clan of Levi. (Ezekiel 43:18–46:24) The holiness of God graces this particular place, this particular time, this particular ritual, this particular person as its embodiment. God the incomprehensible, God who exceeds all human attempts at defining God, wills to be contained within our here and now, within our puny human acts, and even within ourselves.

The construction of space, time, symbols, actions and persons for the performance of religious rituals is the stuff of which priesthood is made. Distinguishable from prophecy, priesthood is also priestcraft, because it is the praxis of evoking and invoking the presence of God. It is a craft of transforming ordinary space into a place of prayer, ordinary time into time for prayer, symbols and actions into rites of prayer. Like a prophet, a priest also engenders hope in new possibilities, but beyond the utterance of "Thus says the LORD." Ezekiel is a priest, and priestly nurturing is part of his ministry to the exiled. "On the banks, on both sides of the river, there will grow all kinds of trees for food. Their leaves will not wither nor their fruit fail, but they will bear fresh fruit every month, because the water for them flows from the sanctuary. Their fruit will be for food, and their leaves for healing." (Ezekiel 47:12)

Religious rituals, whether purification, atonement, cleansing and consecration, or offerings and festivals, transform the significance of human acts as they focus our consciousness to a different dimension of our life. Mundane acts like bathing, sprinkling, sharing the fruits of our labour, sharing a meal, etc., when ritualized, open our mind, heart and soul to the presence of God. What is otherwise worldly and profane shimmers with the holiness of God. "And the name of the city from that time on shall be, The LORD is There." (Ezekiel 48:35b) That God is there – prophesied by the prophet and evoked and invoked by the priest – is reason enough to hope for a homecoming.

Exilic theology, therefore, creates a revolution in our imagination. It transforms our imagination to be attuned – in word and in ritual – to the holiness of God.

A Priestly (P) tradition is part of exilic theology. In fact, it is one current coursing through Scripture. This tradition develops fully at the time of exile. Complementing Ezekiel's priestly caregiving to the exiled, the P tradition leaves its mark in the books of Genesis, Exodus, Leviticus and Numbers. It is called Priestly (P) because it considers the design and creation of space, time, symbols, actions and persons for the liturgy as crucial to rebuilding the broken, exiled community. Unable to change the course of exile, the P tradition releases instead the power of the symbolic, the mythical and the poetic to witness to the holiness, glory and greatness of God, using such literary forms as cultic laws and regulations, genealogies and narratives. The symbolic, the mythical, the poetic have something to say to an exiled people who have nothing more to lose, yet must never relinquish the fire of their own imagination.

The P tradition, in powerfully evocative symbols, refuses to capitulate to the fact of exile. It is a collective act of defiant self-preservation, a fidelity to God despite the eroding global shift of history. It forges a space in the collective consciousness of God's exiled people wherein they may construe a sense of identity. It becomes their only way out of or through their impasse. They remain free despite their bondage.

The priestly imagination, therefore, sets the place, tone, texture, drama, atmosphere, mode and music so that our praying becomes the most appropriate place for the utterance of and reflection on the prophetic word. Severed from the priestly imagination, the prophetic text loses much of its power to inform, to captivate and to mobilize our selves to act as we have imagined. If priestly imagination is this essential, then it requires utmost care.

Priesthood, before it becomes a matter of ordination, is a function of the imagination. Its primary task is not assumption of an office or technical mastery of the finer points of doctrine and rubrics, but mediation of the world of the symbolic, the artistic, the beautiful, the poetic, the sacramental, the enchanting. Its authority lies in a divinely given power to evoke and invoke the presence of God as holy *tremendum et fascinans*: God as at once terrifying and fascinating. Its service lies in its utter self-disposal to the epiphany of the Holy One.

Dedicating a place as a place for prayer, ordaining a time as time for prayer, and consecrating symbols and actions as liturgy, at once honour the immensity of divine mystery, and confess that we nevertheless need it to be within our grasp. The most concrete, material, bodily and sensible becomes a sacrament for the presence and absence of God. The priestly is about sacramentalizing God's presence and absence. Should it forget its role as utterly self-disposing to a divine manifestation, the priestly will reduce itself to mere ritualism. If it usurps the fascinating and terrifying power of the mysterious, the priestly will become demonic desecration. If it relinquishes its gift for the symbolic, the lyrical, the poetic, or its role to protect doctrine and rubric, the priestly will deform itself as dulled symbolic sensitivity.

The priesthood of Ezekiel emerges most properly within this light. Ezekiel beholds the glory of God so that he can speak as prophet and also captivate the people's imagination as a priest. In this regard, his task as priest is best likened to the task of an artist or musician, a poet or dancer. Artists enlarge our imagination so we begin to see that there is more to life than meets the eye, there is more to God than meets our faith. Thus, for Ezekiel, rebuilding the Temple is essential to reconstituting the exiled as God's people once again. A holy place is co-extensive with a people becoming God's holy people. The holiness of God that wills to find its abode *in* the Temple also wills to be present *to* the people. At once localized in a Temple, and absolutely resistant to human manipulation, the holiness of God remains bright, flashing, gleaming, burning, lightning, shining, fire.

We cannot ignore, therefore, the appropriateness of prayer as the sanctuary within which we proclaim and reflect upon Jeremiah, Ezekiel and Second Isaiah. Prayer becomes the setting for engendering a priestly imagination. Were prayer merely textual and bereft of its symbolic matrix, it would hardly be prayer. Were it too rational and too anemic to captivate the imagination, it could not evoke the mystery it is supposed to honour. Were it only an excuse to give vent to uncontrollable emotions, it would not be worship. If it is only strict observance of religous duty, it is not worth doing.

Prayer and, for that matter, liturgy are at their best when they evoke the presence of the mysterious, invoke the mysterious to come, and provoke the response of awe and adoration. We can observe that in Toronto, and perhaps in Canada as a whole, churches of all denominations, or temples, synagogues or mosques, teem with vitality when the immigrant influx is high. We light candles, reverently touch statues and lose ourselves in prayer. Our faces reflect petitions, longing, invocations, cries for help and trust in God.

Places of worship that allow immigrants to express themselves in word and beyond word assist them in their struggle to adapt to a new and different culture. Immigrants add colour, tonal emphasis, excess of gesture, and physical movement to a church's liturgical practice. When marginalized, immigrants create niches of devotional practices that surround the official liturgies. When treated inhospitably, they take their devotional practices elsewhere. When this happens, their entry into mainstream culture becomes more difficult and their acts of worship create ghettoes not only of the mind, but also of the soul.

You have to know what it means to be so broken that all you can do is pray, cling to the rosary, hug the Bible or light a candle. Simply singing a hymn, kneeling or bowing down become acts of self-preservation and cries for help. Here you settle and keep still. Should you be vanquished, at least the enemy – the one outside, or the one within yourself – will not have the ultimate say about your destiny. If this has been your experience, you know the P tradition. You understand the priesthood of Ezekiel. You can appreciate the tradition behind Negro spirituals that can only come from the hearts of the enslaved. Even renaming them as "African-American" spirituals seems to deny the memory of the heartbreak that sparks the song and the singing. You empathize with Native peoples, hoping against hope that their surviving rituals will not be totally banished from their own land. You understand why Filipinos raise their Marian statues and rosaries before the army tanks of a dictator. You realize the poignancy of Jesus' breaking bread and sharing a cup with his disciples on the night he was betrayed.

When priestly acts no longer evoke, our prayers no longer invoke and our liturgies no longer provoke awe and adoration, we risk losing mystery from our lives. When mystery departs, our whole psyche literally plunges into a black hole, pulled by some dark energy that indiscriminately flirts with any seductive purveyor of the spiritual.

A healthy religious ritual orients our entire being to the realm of God's holiness, for whom Ezekiel is the prophet-priest. All rituals – mundane, religious, spiritual and even demonic – are judicious in that they specify within the ritual what is proper, lawful and valid behaviour. All rituals are methodical, because they provide an itinerary, a step-by-step process to approach the desired end. All rituals are dramatic, as they move towards a sense of climax, denouement and closure. All rituals lead the participants from conforming to certain postures, to attentiveness to the shared symbols and their interpretive word, to total engagement in silence and contemplation – yet only the religious ritual distinguishes itself by its ministering to the holiness of God.

In much of contemporary life, especially in First World countries such as Canada, religious ritual is largely overcome by rigorous intellectualizing. Symbols are explained rather than allowed to evoke. People mistrust what is instinctive. Rigorous intellectualizing subtly condescends towards anything devotional, anything that smacks of the ritually idiosyncratic, especially those devotional practices that immigrants take with them. On the other hand, those who have felt suffocated by rigorous intellectualizing experience a deep hunger for what is affectively satisfying and instinctively resonant, venturing into all sorts of spiritualities because church liturgies have become a dead language, the Bible a closed book, religion a prison for their souls. "How could we sing the LORD's song in a foreign land?" (Psalm 137:4)

I often wonder what affects our soul more negatively: the danger of superstition or the danger of rigorous intellectualizing. Before beginning every class I teach, I set up an icon and light a candle; I tell my students that I am simply accommodating to the Filipina in me, and they smile.

Praying is not only invocation, a plea for God to come. It is also evocation, a bringing forth into our consciousness the awareness that the God we have invited is already and always has been there: unnoticed, ignored or even forgotten. Even before we can formulate the words of prayer, and especially when nothing we utter is adequate, lighting a candle, making the sign of the cross, opening the Bible or touching a crucifix can open our consciousness to the religious dimension of our existence. What we touch or listen to or gaze upon enables us to comprehend much more deeply that the uncanny is also the ground of all blessing.

A Prayer Refrain

Place something deeply symbolic of God's presence before you (e.g., a lighted candle, an open Bible, a crucifix) to help you transform ordinary space into prayer space. Assume a prayerful posture, mood and mode.

Call on the Spirit of God to assist you. As you acknowledge that you are enfolded by the presence of God, repeat again and again this prayer: "Holy, holy, holy, LORD God of hosts; the whole earth is full of his glory." (Isaiah 6:3)

Allow this prayer of praise to descend upon you. Let your mind and heart savour it fully. If you are moved to sing, sing a song of praise, again and again, until it becomes a tune you hum.

Be carried by the humming beyond words, to recognize that you are before the holy presence of God. Sustain the last note of the tune like a chant. Chant it until you are transposed into total silence.

Sustain this mode until your eyes open of their own accord. Say "Amen." Continue with the rest of your day.

Do something good for someone to pay homage to that person's life and to God's holiness, glory and greatness.

Priestly acts like this prayer exercise are a way of revering God, who always wants to save. Going beyond the strictures of mere intellectualizing, yet not settling for what is merely emotional or instinctive, priestly acts in the wake of Ezekiel and the P tradition witness to the fullness of divine reality that is at once true, good and beautiful. Whereas the true in God enlightens our mind, and the good in God inspires our will to love, the beautiful in God shines in all glory so that the whole of our being tends towards it in joy and delight. If such splendour becomes as intense as that which Ezekiel beheld, we can only do as Ezekiel did: bow down in worship.

Ministering to the fullness of divine reality in all its truth, goodness and splendour, priestly acts find their home in the poetic, the symbolic, the mythical, the sacramental and the liturgical. We see priestcraft behind the poetic rendition of Creation. (Genesis 1:1–2:4a) It climaxes on the seventh day, which is set aside as a holy day.

The Sabbath changes the people's sense of time. No longer an endless repetition of days, cycles and seasons, time takes on a different orientation. It is open to God who is here now and will forever be. The liturgy of Sabbath observance gives God's people the place and time to "sing the LORD's song in a foreign land." Observing the Sabbath preserves the identity of the exiled against loss and dismemberment. "God blessed the seventh day and hallowed it…." (Genesis 2:3)

To bless is an essential rite of any liturgical event. In the P tradition, blessing is linked to being fruitful, to filling and subduing the earth, and to having dominion over it. Even within and because of the exilic situation of barrenness and subservience, God's holiness that blesses is the only source of hope.

Again and again, spread across the P writings, God extravagantly blesses the whole of Creation. God blesses Noah. (Genesis 8:20–9:17) God blesses Ishmael. (Genesis 21:17–21) God blesses Jacob. (Genesis 35:1–15) God blesses Joseph. (Genesis 48:4) And because God does, the present pain is enfolded by memories of divine blessings in the past as well as hope for more blessings in the future. Past, present and future rest on the holiness of God. Past, present and future are blessed. Past, present and future belong to God because God is the Creator of all that is.

Liturgy enables the exiled to celebrate such an audacious faith against the cruelty of captivity in Babylon. Only within their prayer observances are they able to remember promises fulfilled, and at the same time, anticipate a future when promises will be fulfilled anew. Only within acts of worship can they develop a tradition of construing reality, a tradition that discerns and unabashedly proclaims God at work even in their fallen condition.

Blessing, as God's act of hallowing the whole of Creation, is not an opiate that anaesthetizes a wounded soul. In the P narratives, blessing is as earthy as a promised land, as fleshly as descendants numbered like the stars, and as material as prosperity. When we are landless, barren and poor, we risk too much to hope for a reversal of fortune. We court disaster if such a hope does not rely on God's blessing, if such a hope does not emanate from the holiness of God. Paradoxically, if God, the Creator, hallows the cosmos, then even the place of exile is hallowed. Then it is indeed possible to find prosperity and fruitfulness in the place of exile. We can begin to live what we hope for. The liturgy is the only space where this paradox can be sustained and celebrated.

The world in which P invites God's people to dwell already establishes them in a right relationship with God, the Holy One. It also enables them to take the here and now of exile as the here and now of salvation. The P tradition nurtures a hopeful imagination that anchors the exiled in God's nearness and accessibility without violating God's holiness. The exiled should be faithful to the covenantal relationship with the Holy One. Their shared memory of deliverance from Egypt becomes a promise of future restoration, of a new exodus. Losing land, the exiled find a holy world.

Derailed by the Babylonian sense of world, the exiled commit into the P tradition the conviction that their liturgy is their tent of meeting. Being made aliens, they claim their identity therein. They are no longer exiled because they are, in fact, God's own. They can indeed sing the LORD's song in a foreign land.

What better way of singing is there than worship? Through complex rites of adoration, purification, forgiveness, expiation and sharing a meal, the exiled find a home that is bound and maintained by the holy presence of God in their midst.

A Prayer Exercise

Put yourself in the presence of God. Repeat slowly and reverently "Amen" as many times as you need to, acknowledging and accepting who you are, acknowledging and accepting who God is and what God promises to those who come to pray.

Let the "Amen" define not only your mental posture before God, but also your heart's disposition, your entire being, your recognition of your immigrant condition, even those aspects that you find difficult.

Let the "Amen" be an act of trust in God's gift of home-coming.

Be an "Amen" before God.

If an enlarged sense of peace descends upon you, linger in that grace for a few minutes. Be thankful. It is always good to say "Amen."

Make someone's life better by doing something good for that person.

A coda for the reader

Jeremiah teaches us to pray our grieving. As we allow our grief to puncture our self-containment so that we fall into a seeming abyss, we are handed over to Ezekiel. If Jeremiah is an experience of dissonance, Ezekiel is even more so. His visions of God are terrifying. Ezekiel's passionate God seems too violent for our passionless kind of Christianity. God's assertion of transcendent holiness seems too tyrannical for our dulled Christian taste, too abrasive for our comfortably ordinary religion.

Is the earthquake that is our immigrant experience not enough? Must we be shaken further? So many aspects of our lives are already shifting. We lose our personal bearings. Our own culture reveals its precarious edges. The receiving culture cannot adequately meet us where we long for some experience of God. We are pushed further to consider prayer as our only recourse, yet praying ceases to console.

If we pace our reading of this book so that we can pause to pray, we also pace our entry into our inner selves. We can be slower still as we allow our imagination to become biblical. Such transformation takes time. We join in the liturgical celebrations of our parish with much more attentiveness and involvement. We honour the place of worship in our lives. We honour the revealing and concealing quality of Scripture itself.

Scripture gently opens its world to those who pray it. We minister to others as compassionately as we can. We go on living and praying. The movement from "My joy is gone, grief is upon me, my heart is sick. Hark…" (Jeremiah 8:18–19) to "O dry bones…you shall live" (Ezekiel 37:4–6) is not straightforward. We cannot fast-track from "My God, my God, why have you forsaken me?" (Psalm 22:1) to "Holy, holy, holy, LORD God of hosts; the whole earth is full of his glory." (Isaiah 6:3) There is no shortcut towards being able to say "Amen."

So we gather to pray together or we pray on our own. We set up prayer corners in our homes and offices. We offer to pray for one another or we participate in the official liturgies of the Church. We are exercising our priesthood as the baptized in Christ. Though our sense of the holy is more instinctive than academically trained, such a sense is trustworthy. As we perform priestly acts of blessing, propitiation, intercession, invocation, offering, sacrifice and adoration, we construe a far richer, more colourful, more engaging, more evocative, more prayerful world. Within that world we can stand before the many disjunctions of our life and await the Lord.

Mystics of the Christian tradition attest that at the anagogical moment they experience God on the physical-psychological level. What Christians hold in faith, mystics experience as physically and psychologically real. Mystics across the centuries have given this experience different names, but they have consistently warned us that we cannot make this happen on our own, nor should we be disappointed if such a psycho-physical event is not given to us.

Not all of us can be mystics, but all of us are capable of contemplation. Our faithful and total attentiveness to our selves, our surroundings, our inner world and a larger reality exceeds our tendency to bend this total reality to our will. We contemplate in faith that beyond what our mind can configure is God's mysterious, fascinating, terrifying presence, and we give this presence the honour and praise that is due the Holy One. Contemplation is our being totally present to God. It is, therefore, a presence unto Presence. It is not the sole preoccupation of nuns and monks enclosed in monastery walls. In the final analysis, it is a basic stance towards life that emerges slowly in and as a result of prayer. "O dry bones…you shall live." (Ezekiel 37:4–6)

References

Walter Brueggemann. "The Kerygma of the Priestly Writers." *The Vitality of the Old Testament Traditions*, Walter Brueggemann and Hans Walter Wolff, eds. Atlanta: John Knox Press, 1975.

Aelred Cody, O.S.B. *Ezekiel with an Excursus on Old Testament Priesthood.* Wilmington, DE: Michael Glazier, Inc., 1984.

Philip Peter Jensen. *Graded Holiness: A Key to the Priestly Conception of the World.* Journal for the Study of the Old Testament, Supplement Series 106, David J.A. Clines and Philip R. Davies, eds. Sheffield, England: JSOT Press, 1992.

Paul Joyce. *Divine Initiative and Human Response in Ezekiel.* Journal for the Study of the Old Testament, Supplement Series, David J.A. Clines and Philip R. Davies, eds. Sheffield, England: JSOT Press, 1989.

Paul J. Philibert, OP. "Readiness for Ritual: Psychological Aspects of Maturity in Christian Celebration." *Alternative Futures for Worship, Volume I,* Regis A. Duffy, OFM et al, eds. Collegeville, MN: The Liturgical Press, 1987: 63–122.

Bruce Vawter and Leslie J. Hoppe. *A New Heart: A Commentary on the Book of Ezekiel.* Grand Rapids, MI: Eerdmans, 1991.

Second Isaiah Offers a Vision of Homecoming

"Comfort, O comfort my people, says your God." (Isaiah 40:1) God comes to bring us home. Instead of rushing to transform this idea of home into a huge suburban house with a two-door garage financed with a six-figure income, we allow Second Isaiah to hold our imagination captive as he poetically draws a theological geography of home. His poetry is commonly dated circa 550 BCE, just as the Babylonian empire is about to collapse in the face of rising Persian power.

Biblical scholars conclude that there are enough reasons in the text to differentiate the authorship of Isaiah 40–55 from the first part of the book, chapters 1 to 39, and the last part, chapters 56 to 66. So they speak of Isaiah, Second Isaiah and Third Isaiah, ordering them chronologically, with Isaiah as pre-exilic, Second Isaiah as exilic, and Third Isaiah as post-exilic. Traditions of editing place all these layers of prophetic work under the name of the prophet Isaiah, the prophet of chapters 1 to 39, while leaving the other two unnamed. Nevertheless, biblical scholars theorize that these two unnamed prophets belong to the Isaian prophetic tradition.

Second Isaiah crafts a poetry of homecoming against an exilic backdrop. Engendering hope among the hopeless, the prophet offers the exiled a way through their dark night when all they feel is a sense of resignation to an irrevocable reality.

A vision that begins with hope

Though the theme of hope also runs through Jeremiah and Ezekiel, it is Second Isaiah who is most identified with it. By the time Second Isaiah comes on the scene, God's exiled people have already given up on being able to go home. So the kind of hoping Second Isaiah arouses among them is not mere bravado or blind optimism. It is hope that knows despair. It is hope that has seen too much and has known too many heart-aches. It is hope for a homecoming that can only come from God.

In turning to Second Isaiah, therefore, we remain at a point of hunger and need for the language of grief, for a way of coming to terms with God's seeming absence, and also for a vision of a homecoming.

"Comfort, O comfort my people, says your God." (Isaiah 40:1) The kind of hope Second Isaiah nurtures is one that looks to God without binding God to human expectations. This is difficult on two counts. First, the people are at the point when even a Job would have ceased to ask his questions, when even a Jeremiah would have given up lamenting – "But Zion said, 'The LORD has forsaken me, my LORD has forgotten me.'" (Isaiah 49:14) Second, they have settled for the inevitable. What else is there? Really? "Can the prey be taken from the mighty, or the captives of a tyrant be rescued?" (Isaiah 49:24)

It is the task of Second Isaiah to provoke the people's collective imagination to dream differently, to go against the flat and prosaic practicality of the day-to-day. Second Isaiah must spark a hopeful imagination amid the darkness of their disappointments, when there seems to be no longer any point to grieving, and when God seems to be too wholly Other to reverse the course of history – "My way is hidden from the LORD, and my right is disregarded by my God." (Isaiah 40:27)

A hopeful imagination is not only about hope; it is also about a particular envisioning of homecoming. Hope is a risky venture because it demands vulnerability. How vulnerable can a hard-nosed realist be? To hope vulnerably, they must listen for a different heartbeat, one that throbs according to God's own sense of rhythm. More than this, homecoming in God is a musical score different from the exiled's compositions of home. Second Isaiah must contend with the inertia and passivity of the exiled as well as their inability to imagine what homecoming in God could be. "Comfort, O comfort my people, says your God." (Isaiah 40:1)

Grieving with Jeremiah is not merely grieving the loss of land, Temple, king and priesthood; it is grieving a much more primordial loss, the loss of a sense of God. The holiness of God, as the basis for the return to the land, for the restoration of the Temple, the kingdom and the priesthood, uncompromisingly sets in bold relief that, for Ezekiel, there is no real homecoming apart from God. Like Jeremiah and Ezekiel before him, Second Isaiah unabashedly proclaims that exile is a theological issue. Homecoming, as well, is primarily a theological reality. Second Isaiah sustains this fundamental theme. In this light, immigrants will have to configure their own homecoming in a foreign land.

A vision that invites appropriation by immigrants

How can immigrants insert themselves into the Isaian text? We can only do so if we are willing to yield wholly to God our kind of exile and our own hope for a homecoming. Every other consequence, expectation and intention implied in this yielding will be secondary. We pray our way to a homecoming in a foreign land. We invest a total trust in the power of prayer to assist us in making that come about.

If this proves to be too much investment on something as seemingly insubstantial as prayer, and we turn away, we will not be the first to do so. What is offered here is no magic potion to wipe out the bruises of immigrant life. There is no precaution to lessen the seismic shifts that immigrants suffer. There is no instant miracle cure for immigrant affliction. Nor is there a comprehensive strategic plan for immigrant homecoming in a foreign land.

Jeremiah, Ezekiel and Second Isaiah can speak to our immigrant condition. We can listen to them in the context of prayer and configure the homecoming that can be granted us.

"Comfort, O comfort my people, says your God." (Isaiah 40:1) The poetry of Isaiah 40–55 bursts forth in images meant to awaken a collective imagination that has become lethargic in captivity. Subdued by the seeming permanence of exile, God's people are enlivened by reminders of the pulsating immensity of creation and the greater immensity of God as Creator. Poetic symphonies of triumph, freedom, conquest, victory, joy, exultation and the glory of God deluge their senses, flattened as they are by the monotony of Babylon. Rendered guilty, but now forgiven and redeemed, the exiled receive a sure promise of a homecoming that both subverts and exceeds their expectations – "Every valley shall be lifted up, and every mountain and hill be made low; the uneven ground shall become level, and the rough places a plain. Then the glory of the LORD shall be revealed." (Isaiah 40:4–5a)

The unmistakably theocentric thrust of Second Isaiah echoes Ezekiel and Jeremiah. Turn to God, and you will come home. God turns towards you. You are home.

Inaugurated by chapter 40, and repeated in the subsequent chapters, the theocentric pull of Second Isaiah's poetry sustains the unflinching fidelity of the prophets of exile to their vocation. Our faithful insertion of our immigrant lives into their prophetic text, through the *lectio divina*, assures us of the beginning of our own homecoming.

A *Lectio Divina* on Isaiah 40:1-11

Lectio

Read and reread the text until it permeates your entire being. Then focus on the line "Comfort, O comfort my people, says your God." (Isaiah 40:1)

Meditatio

God calls the prophet "to speak tenderly to Jerusalem." (Isaiah 40:2a) Like Ezekiel, Second Isaiah, the herald of good tidings, witnesses to the glory of God. The prophet calls the people to "prepare the way of the LORD" (Isaiah 40:3a), for then "the glory of the LORD shall be revealed." (Isaiah 40:5a) Though the exiled may be like grass that withers or a flower that easily fades, God will stand forever in constancy. (Isaiah 40:6-8) At the centre of Second Isaiah's theological geography of home is God, the LORD, the Holy One of Israel, Creator and Redeemer, the first and the last, the Only God:

"Here is your God!"
See, the LORD God comes with might,
and his arm rules for him;
his reward is with him,
and his recompense before him.
He will feed his flock like a shepherd;
he will gather the lambs in his arms,
and carry them in his bosom,
and gently lead the mother sheep.
(Isaiah 40:9c–11)

God assaults our presumptions of who and what God is:

Who has measured the waters in the hollow of his hand
and marked off the heavens with a span,
enclosed the dust of the earth in a measure,
and weighed the mountains in scales
and the hills in a balance?
Who has directed the spirit of the LORD,
or as his counsellor has instructed him?
Whom did he consult for his enlightenment,
and who taught him the path of justice?
Who taught him knowledge,
and showed him the way of understanding?
(Isaiah 40:12–14)

God goes on and on toppling down all our mental, ideo-
logical, imagistic, psychological, emotional and moral prisms
that distort our understanding. "To whom then will you liken
God, or what likeness compare with him?" (Isaiah 40:18)

The theological point of exile is to know who God is, and
who we really are before God – "a drop from a bucket; dust on
the scales; nothing and emptiness." (Isaiah 40:15–17)

The liveliness and boldness of God in the poetry of Second
Isaiah should be enough to shake us out of the habitual stupor
with which we approach Scripture in prayer and in liturgy.
God has become so equated with words that God is readily

parsed, exegeted, managed, deconstructed, distorted and eventually dismissed.

A prayerful disposition that has passed through the crucible of disjunctions becomes a guard against this all too human tendency to reduce God into bite-size pieces. Prayer that is open to Scripture's revelatory power reveres the inviolable space for God's holiness.

> Have you not known? Have you not heard?
> The LORD is the everlasting God,
>   the Creator of the ends of the earth.
> He does not faint or grow weary;
>   his understanding is unsearchable.
> He gives power to the faint,
>   and strengthens the powerless.
> *(Isaiah 40:28–29)*

In prayer it happens (we do not know how) that the words we read suddenly give way to an almost palpable presence of God. Then we can only gently capitulate to this all-encompassing reality that draws close to us. We dwell in each other as in a tent of meeting.

> But you, Israel, my servant,
>   Jacob, whom I have chosen,
> the offspring of Abraham, my friend;
> you whom I took from the ends of the earth,
>   and called from its farthest corners,
> saying to you, "You are my servant,
> I have chosen you and not cast you off";
>   do not fear, for I am with you,
>   do not be afraid, for I am your God;
> I will strengthen you, I will help you,
> I will uphold you with my victorious right hand.
> *(Isaiah 41:8–10)*

Loss remains loss, but now it becomes relative to a fullness that promises another beginning. Tears of grieving meld with tears of joy, because in this moment of indwelling, comfort and consolation enfold us like a motherly embrace. Displacement finds anchor in God. The gaping ache inside meets a fundamentally graced resolve to be totally open and present to one's reality. We can almost touch this blessing that extravagantly grants us the courage to be, no matter what else may happen. Our feet, which have been straddling two worlds, land on solid ground. The tightness in our gut, the shortness of our breath, the knot in our throat – in short, our existential unease – trustingly release into an enfolding welcome. Discordant feelings begin to dance to a primordial rhythm in God who, after all, continually hovers over our chaos. We lucidly see the right thing to do here and now, and we consequently invest ourselves wholly to do that right thing.

Even after this moment fades, something irrevocably lingers. Perceptions of being caught between a door and a door jamb, of being a small fish in big pond, no longer grip the mind. We are less prone to wallow in self-pity. We are less likely to follow the path of least resistance, or to vent our wounded anger.

The contemplative moment in prayer graces us with intimate knowing. We know God, the IS, as I AM WITH YOU. The One who is strength and help overcomes our fear, disbelief, intellectual reserve, apprehension, grasping manipulation. By the same token, God as I AM WITH YOU upholds us so that as our fear, unbelief, reserve, apprehension and grasping manipulation are overcome, we do not succumb to the other extreme of mental dis-ease, emotional frenzy and loss of common sense. We are never as totally awake, aware and attentive as at this moment. God knows us. We are Israel. We are Jacob. We are chosen.

As we are plunged into intimate knowing, we do not lose ourselves in a self-enclosed beatitude. Rather, beatitude is becoming what God has chosen us to be: God's servant and friend. Contemplation is intrinsically connected with the life of service, with raw engagement with day-to-day reality.

> When the poor and needy seek water,
> and there is none,
> and their tongue is parched with thirst,
> I the LORD will answer them,
> I the God of Israel will not forsake them.
> *(Isaiah 41:17)*

The intent of praying our way towards a homecoming is to find rest in this sure knowledge of God. Then we can sing the LORD's song in a foreign land. "Sing to the LORD a new song, his praise from the end of the earth" (Isaiah 42:10a), "sing, O heavens" (Isaiah 44:23), "sing for joy" (Isaiah 49:13), "sing, O barren one." (Isaiah 54:1)

God's comfort makes us sing. Second Isaiah reprises his theme and sub-themes again and again. God desires to comfort. God asserts God's sovereignty. God reproaches Judah for their unfaithfulness. God calls them home. The words fall like gentle rain on a parched desert earth. In chapter 43, we have the downpour. In staccato beat, God overwhelms exiled Judah:

> Do not fear, for I have redeemed you;
> I have called you by name, you are mine.
> *(Isaiah 43:1b)*

> When you pass through the waters, I will be with you....
> *(Isaiah 43:2a)*

> For I am the LORD your God,
> the Holy One of Israel, your Saviour....
> *(Isaiah 43:3a)*

[Y]ou are precious in my sight, and honoured,
and I love you.
(Isaiah 43:4a)

Do not fear for I am with you.
(Isaiah 43:5a)

I, I am the LORD, and besides me there is no saviour.
(Isaiah 43:11)

I am God, and also henceforth I am He;
there is no one who can deliver from my hand;
I work and who can hinder it?
(Isaiah 43:13)

I am the LORD, your Holy One,
the Creator of Israel, your King.
(Isaiah 43:15)

The God who speaks tenderly to the exiled
is our God, too. Let us turn to the one who says
Do not fear for I am with you.
(Isaiah 43:5a)

Oratio

Give yourself freedom to express everything to God.

Contemplatio

After you have poured yourself out, rest on one word that encapsulates your prayer (e.g., trust, surrender, hope, confident waiting, humility, being present, "help!", "why?", lament). Assume that word wholly. Don't *think* the word, *be* the word; don't *feel* the word, *be* the word. Be.

If an enlarged sense of peace descends upon you, linger in that grace for a few minutes. Be thankful. Be resolute to be more attentive and responsible for your situation. It is always good to say "Amen."

Concretely respond to the summons "Comfort, O comfort my people, says your God." (Isaiah 40:1)

So that our immigrant story becomes our story with God

Exile paves the way for homecoming. Immigrants *will* find a home in a foreign land. Though we cannot decide beforehand what such a homecoming will be, right now, right here, we can trust that it is God, the Creator of heaven and earth, who remains the Lord of our life and of our history. Our immigrant story takes on the added theme of being our story with God. Telling our immigrant story also becomes a narrative of what God has done for us.

> Thus says the LORD,
> who makes a way in the sea,
> and a path in the mighty waters,
> who brings out chariot and horse,
> army and warrior;
> they lie down, they cannot rise,
> they are extinguished, quenched like a wick:
> Do not remember the former things,
> or consider the things of old.
> I am about to do a new thing;
> now it springs forth, do you not perceive it?
> I will make a way in the wilderness
> and rivers in the desert.
> The wild animals will honor me,
> the jackals and the ostriches;
> for I give water in the wilderness,
> rivers in the desert,
> to give drink to my chosen people,
> the people whom I have formed myself
> so that they might declare my praise.
> *(Isaiah 43:16–21)*

God is our only source of strength, and God will take us home. Our geography of loss, of disorientation, and of hope for a homecoming becomes God's place of abiding.

If something like this happens to us when we pray, praying ceases to be merely one of those things we do. Praying becomes foundational. It cannot be viewed as a luxury, nor can anything else take its rightful place in our life. Praying undergirds everything for which we assume responsibility. It cannot compete with other activities. If we start screaming at the kids to be quiet (can't they see we are praying?), then prayer has not yet become a still point from which we dispense our energy for living. If, after a weekend retreat, we dread the drive back home, then praying has not yet become a habit of mindfulness. Born out of discipline and faithfulness, praying creates a rhythm of inwardness and outwardness. We can no longer complain about it taking our time, because we cannot be without it.

> But now hear, O Jacob my servant,
> Israel whom I have chosen!
> Thus says the LORD who made you,
> who formed you in the womb and will help you:
> Do not fear, O Jacob my servant.
> *(Isaiah 44:1–2)*

Praying like this creates a pattern of reflection–action–reflection. We move inward, into ourselves, to find a centre that can hold in tension the many stress-filled dispersions, painful disjunctions, overwhelming incongruencies and humiliating inconsistencies that make our immigrant life. All the while, aided by the prophets of exile, we open this centre to God. The *lectio divina* places us on the threshold where the One who says, "Do not fear O Jacob my servant" (Isaiah 44:1a) will become so irresistibly real that we can only respond "Amen."

We rest upon this threshold with only our openness and the biblical text as life support. And this is enough. The text establishes a larger framework within which our sense of loss, our disorientation and our hope for homecoming are like a river flowing into the sea. We move out of prayer, better able to move into the many demands of our lives.

We can therefore weave the varied strands of our immigrant life – the old and the new, our homesickness, our disorientation, our successes and our failures, our inroads into mainstream culture and our cultural peculiarities, our concern for fellow immigrants, our dislocation, our fondness for our own food or music, our devotional practices – into a fabric of meaning, the completion of which we may not see. The incompleteness no longer baffles. The incongruities and inconsistencies no longer perturb. Prayer grants us the insight that God, in God's immanence and transcendence, oversees an ongoing and never quite finished project.

> Thus says the LORD, your Redeemer,
> who formed you in the womb:
> I am the LORD, who made all things,
> who alone stretched out the heavens,
> who by myself spread out the earth;
> who frustrates the omens of liars,
> and makes fools of diviners;
> who turns back the wise,
> and makes their knowledge foolish;
> who confirms the word of his servant,
> and fulfills the prediction of his messengers;
> who says of Jerusalem, "It shall be inhabited,"
> and of the cities of Judah, "They shall be rebuilt,
> and I will raise up their ruins."
> *(Isaiah 44:24–26)*

Homecoming is not simply a return to our land of birth, nor is it complete integration into our land of adoption. While "home" may still tug at our hearts, we are also trying to settle down in a foreign country. The home where memory resides is in our land of origin. The home that hope looks towards is our land of adoption. Either way we exist at their margins. We grasp the edges of both our memory and our hoping. Between them is this chasm of homelessness. Right here in this chasm, as we pray, we are gifted with the knowledge of a homecoming in God. And here, in in-betweenness, we sew our quilt of meaning, and wait for what is still to come.

Some of us, upon retirement, may decide to go back to our land of birth, where we can enjoy the fruits of our forays in a foreign land. Others choose the final symbolic act of being buried at home, obeying the pull of their native land and desiring the final embrace of their native soil. But in the meantime, we stay in the land of adoption, always feeling in-between north and south, east and west.

We may succeed in crossing an invisible cultural barrier, and therefore no longer feel like an outsider. We expand the cultural base of our adopted land, which includes us, not only by legal edict but also by its para-rational, even visceral, sense of identification. Yet, as long as we are a minority, as long as we still have a thick accent, so long as the colour of our skin or the shape of our eyes and nose makes us look different from the Caucasian norm, we are still caught between north and south, east and west.

Therefore, if this in-betweenness is where we discern God's abiding, then this is home for us. Anywhere else is not truly home. We can only endure if we imagine such an awesome world the way Scripture imagines it. We begin to also perceive our here and now in a new way, because we realize that we always and essentially are in God. If God is our ultimate home, we will always be in exile on earth.

In-betweenness is the crack in the wall, through which we perceive not only the tenuousness of our own sense of home, but also the inexhaustibility of other possibilities that come from God. In-betweenness becomes a habitable world.

Listen to me, O house of Jacob,
all the remnant of the house of Israel,
who have been borne by me from your birth,
carried from the womb;
even to your old age I am he,
even when you turn gray I will carry you.
I have made, and I will bear;
I will carry and will save.

(Isaiah 46:3–4)

The long journey home begins with a revolution in our imagination. This is an imagination – at once biblical, prayerful and priestly – that thrives on the images (or counter-images) offered by Jeremiah, Ezekiel and Second Isaiah. As we receive the proclaimed Word from the prophets of exile, we are also handed over to the Word. A captivated imagination generates its own energy to live as it has imagined.

Am I home? Even theologically, it takes a lifetime to reach the shore.

I believe that prayer can have real effects on our lives, especially if it finds its language in the biblical theology of exile. I cannot account for all the ramifications. What I offer is a limited perspective, and a cartography that requires us to take a similar journey on our own. The performative nature of the enterprise has less to do with map-reading than with taking the step towards unexplored dimensions of prayer, which is, after all, a movement towards being present not only to God, not only to oneself, but to our shared, everyday world.

See, I have refined you, but not like silver;
I have tested you in the furnace of adversity.
For my own sake, for my own sake, I do it,
for why should my name be profaned?
My glory I will not give to another.

(Isaiah 48:10–11)

The cartography of the immigrant experience as exile is not a substitute for actual prayerful passage toward a closer relationship with God. Neither can it guarantee a direct experience of God.

God is God, who remains the wholly Other, who gratuitously may come as unmediated presence. This is God's own prerogative. It is also God's prerogative to mediate God's holy presence through everything in the created order. It has been God's prerogative to enter human history so that nothing will ever separate us from God's love. So we take our concrete existence and hallow everything we experience there, because these experiences are sacraments of God's intimate presence to us and to all reality.

This prayerful reflection on the immigrant experience cannot guarantee worldly success either, as if by assiduous performance of the prayers here, we will end up totally mainstreamed, or better, upstreamed, complete with a cottage in Muskoka. It cannot guarantee that all problems will disappear, that there will be justice for the oppressed, that we will return to the land, that we will rebuild the Temple, that the kingdom will be restored, and that we will all live happily ever after.

This prayerful reflection on the immigrant experience witnesses to the reliability of biblical faith to steer our life towards a self-revealing God. From the beginning, and through time, God has willed to be known, and has cared that, indeed, we find prosperity, we return to the land, we rebuild the Temple, we bring about justice, we live happily ever after. But as well, biblical faith is uncompromising in its insistence that all that we wish remain secondary to our fidelity to God. All these things are not automatic consequences of our faith in God.

This prayerful reflection on the immigrant experience enables us to enter the world of Scripture, our own inner world, and the fundamentally holy ground of our existence so that we can enter more fully into our shared humanity. It helps us identify with biblical characters and their fate. We are Israel. We are Jacob.

We do not take a fundamentalist approach to Scripture, an approach that glosses over our geographical, temporal and cultural difference from it. Nor do we negate Scripture's own original context, overriding it with our own current existential need, or highlight Scripture's moral lessons so that we dispose of Scripture like a husk once we have drawn its grain. We do not demythologize Scripture, dispensing of it like a prop after we are catapulted into a personal and existential encounter with our own selves.

This imaginative leap takes seriously the task of exegesis and the summons to pray Scripture. We move through the senses of Scripture, while informed by the findings of biblical scholarship, so we can be at that juncture when the words and the self-revealing God of Scripture engage us. Moving towards the anagogical, we respond to God's invitation to a covenantal relationship. Then we become part of God's people. We are Israel. We are Jacob. Their story is our story. Their ancestors become our ancestors. Their destiny in God becomes ours as well. The crests and troughs of their story with God — exile to Babylon and exodus, wandering in the desert, forging the covenant, establishing the kingdom, homecoming, becoming a remnant of *anawim* or the poorest of the poor — also shape our own storylines. Their sins are our sins. Their unfaithfulness is our unfaithfulness. The grace given them is the grace given us as well.

> Thus says the LORD:
> In a time of favour I have answered you,
> on a day of salvation I have helped you;
> I have kept you and given you
> as a covenant to the people,
> to establish the land,

> to apportion the desolate heritages;
> saying to the prisoners, "Come out,"
> to those who are in darkness, "Show yourselves."
> *(Isaiah 49:8–9a)*

This imaginative identification that allows us to own the originating story exists within Scripture itself. As they help God's people deal with their situation in Babylon, the prophets of exile are the custodians of the people's memory. Lest exile make the Israelites forget, the prophets continually bring to mind what God has done for them since the beginning.

So that our story with God becomes a tradition of remembrance

The condition of exile develops a tradition of remembrance that brings the past to bear on the present sorrow, so that within such sorrow, the exiled can envision an open future laden with new possibilities. "Look to Abraham your father and to Sarah who bore you; for he was but one when I called him, but I blessed him and made him many." (Isaiah 51:2)

Biblical scholars name this tradition of remembrance "Deuteronomist." Behind this tradition, they posit a historian (or community of historians) who, in the midst of exilic loss, calls to mind the history of God's chosen people – not to make the exiled find solace in the past, but to enable them to live history as an ongoing story. Even in their bleak here and now, the God of their history remains their God and continues to forge a story among them: this is a God who will never forget God's own.

The Deuteronomist tradition dramatizes history as ongoing story in the books of Deuteronomy, Joshua, Judges, 1 and 2 Samuel, and 1 and 2 Kings. Prominent in this tradition of remembrance are its heroes: Moses, Joshua, Samuel and Solomon, who address the exiled in their present pain. The story of

God's people has a pattern of infidelity followed by forgiveness. If they return to God, they will come home. The covenant will be the basis of homecoming. They must set their hearts to come home. They are to be re-membered back to God. The tradition of remembrance is not merely a guard against forgetfulness, it is also an attempt to heal dismemberment from God.

The return to memory is not a tedious spinning of the wheel – what goes up must come down; what goes around, comes around. Nor is it merely living through a change in seasons – winter, spring, summer, fall. In their liturgy, and in the retelling of their story as God's people, the exiled renew their faith in the God who promises to do something new. Exhausted and impoverished by their present displacement, they are reminded, in ritual and in story, of God's inexhaustible power. Remembering and re-membered, the exiled will be God's people once again. Remembering and re-membered, the exiled will be God's witnesses to the ends of the earth.

The Deuteronomist tradition of remembrance is foreign to the contemporary mind, which looks at history in a linear way and seeks factual precision, complete with social, political, economic, deconstructionist analysis. Such a stance makes the biblical sense of history look embellished, albeit well-meaning, whose value lies in the realm of the merely metaphorical, or morally didactic, or exhortative or inspirational. Yet the Deuteronomist tradition makes a bold truth claim about the reliability of God so that right now, in exile, homecoming becomes a certainty.

The Deuteronomist tradition is not a familiar one in Filipino culture. It is a peculiarly biblical way of invoking God's presence among the exiled through their history. For us to embrace this tradition as our own is a theological act of appropriation, an imaginative leap born out of prayer.

It is obvious now that God's comfort is more than consolation, more than propping up pillows so we can rest and forget about our loss, our dislocation, our homesickness, our many uneasy compromises. Comfort from God is not an analgesic. Comfort is knowing God as I AM WITH YOU. God is there when our world breaks apart. God is there when things do not work out the way we would have wished. God is there when we are overcome and overwhelmed. God is there in our crises of loss and disorientation. God is there as we hope. We can turn to God. We can believe God's constancy cradles our homelessness. Being uprooted, we become, paradoxically, rooted in God's awesome transcendence.

Hadewijch, the medieval Flemish Beguine, describes the life of prayer as an inverted tree whose roots reach out into eternity. This image captures the immigrant search for home and the tension inherent in the natural tendency of roots to grasp and take firm hold of the ground. It pictures uprootedness and inability to immediately reroot in unfamiliar territory, and a prayerful, straining openness to God as the ultimate basis for a homecoming in a foreign land.

Try to assume this image existentially and you will discover how you inwardly recoil in terror over the prospect of having to totally trust the ungraspable, how your whole being tightens and curls unto itself like a caterpillar that twines itself around the end of the twig because it does not have wings to fly. What John of the Cross calls the dark night of the soul, the French philosopher Albert Camus calls the absurd. The rest of us, who resist the precariousness of our seemingly secure world, are happy not to think about it.

"Comfort, O comfort my people, says your God." (Isaiah 40:1) We insert ourselves into the biblical story. We graft ourselves onto the Deuteronomist tradition of remembrance so that our homecoming in a foreign land may also be a theological event, a profession of faith that the God of Jeremiah, Ezekiel and Second Isaiah is also our God, who brings us back, who re-members us to God's own self. The biblical language of our immigrant soul grants us a habitable world that securely grounds our concrete space-and-time existence in remembering and being re-membered.

> Enlarge the site of your tent,
> and let the curtains of your habitations be stretched out;
> do not hold back;
> lengthen your cords,
> and strengthen your stakes.
> For you will spread out to the right and to the left,
> and your descendants will possess the nations
> and will settle the desolate towns.
> *(Isaiah 54:2–3)*

We cannot sensibly trust in such a promise of a homecoming in God if we do not receive it in prayer. We do not appreciate prayer more than when it is the only thing that matters, the only thing that keeps us going, the only thing that can sustain our sanity, especially when we helplessly watch what is safe and secure – home – crumble before our eyes. We must be this desperate to expect so much from praying, that we stretch ourselves beyond superficiality and habit into the One who makes it prayer. It is God who comes to meet us.

> For as the rain and the snow come down from heaven,
> and do not return there until they have watered the earth,
> making it bring forth and sprout,
> giving seed to the sower and bread to the eater,
> so shall my word be that goes out from my mouth;
> it shall not return to me empty,
> but it shall accomplish that which I purpose,
> and succeed in the thing for which I sent it.
> *(Isaiah 55:10–11)*

As we allow Jeremiah, Ezekiel and Second Isaiah to minister to us as immigrants, we find a theological language for our soul. Though we do not intend to wrestle into words what may always be unspoken and unspeakable in our immigrant experience, we do want to name it, so that by naming it, it may cease to be meaningless and absurd. The biblical theology of exile is a perspective that grants understanding. Where culture clash makes our view of our world unbalanced, the biblical theology of exile helps us discern God at work, in spite of everything.

So that we can minister

Naming is a way of understanding. Jeremiah, Ezekiel and Second Isaiah educate us to perceive God in our immigrant condition. What appears hopeless becomes a possible ground for a theophany – a visible manifestation of God. We are granted the courage to face our situation, and not be paralyzed by fear or despair.

In Jeremiah, grieving over our loss directs our gaze away from our sorrow towards God. Instead of wallowing in negative self-preoccupation provoked by grief, we pour ourselves out to God. In Ezekiel, our childish and culturally based notions of God break down before God's utterly transcendent holiness – bright, flashing, gleaming, burning, lightning, shining, fire. In Second Isaiah, God, the Transcendent One, becomes as immanent as home.

As we name, we see. As we see, we pray. As we pray, we act. Isaiah 40–55 occasions an encounter with the enigmatic Suffering Servant of the LORD. Though the exact length of the Servant poems remains an issue among scholars, they seem to agree that these poems are found in Isaiah 42:1–7, 49:1–7, 50:4–9 and 52:13–53:12. The Servant is a "chosen one" called to fulfill the role of both the Davidic king and the messianic king. The Servant brings about justice quietly. The Servant's weakness displays strength. Like

Jeremiah, the Suffering Servant is a sorrowing person of faith who learns to seek consolation solely in the LORD. The Servant remains one with people in sorrow and yet distinct from them in innocence of life and total service of God.

> I am the LORD, I have called you in righteousness,
> I have taken you by the hand and kept you;
> I have given you as a covenant to the people,
> a light to the nations,
> to open the eyes that are blind,
> to bring out the prisoners from the dungeon,
> from the prison those who sit in darkness.
> *(Isaiah 42:6–7)*

Though Christian appropriation automatically equates the Suffering Servant of the LORD to Christ, biblical scholars are more careful to highlight that the Servant is not one particular person but Judah itself, God's chosen one who, in the dark night of its history, is called to be the light of all the nations; Judah, in its exilic state, is summoned not only to return to God, but also to be more mindful of its "widows and orphans," of aliens in its midst (Deuteronomy 42:17–18), than it is of its own wounds. Suffering makes one self-centred. Judah, as the Suffering Servant, is called to be selfless because its contemplation of God results in compassion for those suffering in its midst.

Before the economics, politics and sociology of struggle sway us, it would be well to pause and pursue the implication of being called to minister to others – not from our bounty, but from our poverty; not from our power, but from our powerlessness; not from our success, but from our failure. We are to give when there seems to be nothing to give; we are to offer strength from our sense of depletion; and we are to show love despite our loneliness.

And he said to me, "You are my servant,
Israel, in whom I will be glorified."
But I said, "I have laboured in vain,
I have spent my strength for nothing and vanity;
yet surely my cause is with the LORD,
and my reward with my God."
(Isaiah 49:3–4)

If existing ethnic communities do not provide immigrants with a support system that facilitates adjustment to the new country, it is as if we have been thrown overboard into inhospitable waters. Our insignificant lives are lost in the sea of our host country's history, the beginning of which we do not share, and the ongoing events of which we do not comprehend. Before advocacy groups and aid centres locate our presence on the larger political map, complete with statistics and social analysis, we feel small, disconnected, forgotten and dispensable. From this vantage point, we will have an appreciation of what it means to be Suffering Servant. Yet, from here we nevertheless offer to be of service.

Eventually, we gather close together in a neighbourhood so that city street names are translated in our language. Certain services and trades are identified with our ethnic faces. We amass strength to protest the atrocities committed against our country of origin, and we influence political correctness to fine-tune language in reference to us. The dominant culture hesitates to offend our feelings and sensitivities. Bookstores and libraries allot a section to studies about us. When these things happen, we already are one step beyond the suffering of the Suffering Servant of the LORD. By then, we have some power, some financial resources, and a mobilized community as support system. We cannot be bullied back into insignificance. Can you imagine how much hurt and anger will simmer if that were to happen again? Could love come at all from utter desolation?

Yet the Suffering Servant is innocent of human folly and sinfulness. The Servant's suffering is not a form of futile dereliction, inflicted out of sheer unthinking self-destructiveness, or out of mere cowardice, loss of nerve and passive aggression. In three places, chapter 42 of the first Servant Song mentions justice as a correlate of God's own righteousness and the covenant of faithfulness. The innocent sufferer puts the whole of reality in its just relationship as ordained by God, and refuses to continue the cycle of vengeful anger that eventually leads into unstoppable bloodletting. The one who does justice suffers. Whoever stops killing for the sake of justice will die. This is the Lamb of God who takes away the sins of the world.

The Suffering Servant forgives. Forgiveness is one of the hardest decisions to follow through on because we have been sinned against, violated, run over. The deeper the violation, the more helpless we become. We have no energy left to be indignant or to lash out in vengeance. We become victims, without any power to resist aggression, and without any desire to compound the aggression with our own.

Forgiveness goes beyond the requirements of justice. Forgiveness begins with our decision not to be deformed by violence. Forgiveness moves us beyond the gridlock of conflict, towards a more encompassing space within ourselves that is beyond the claws of the negative intimacy between fear and anger.

In the Catholic understanding of the soul's anatomy, that more encompassing space is where we retain God's image, which is not only inviolable, but is also the inexhaustible source of love. As we allow that love to conquer our fear, we will cease to internalize the other's anger. We will see it for what it is, someone else's anger.

Forgiveness can lead to healing of the other's anger. Forgiveness fathoms the underlying inadequacies that anger has masked. Forgiveness grants those inadequacies acceptance and understanding. The other can be invited to hand those inadequacies to God, from whom all forgiveness and love emanate.

Forgiveness gives both victim and victimizer another chance. But the aggressor can only ask for forgiveness. It is the victim's prerogative to grant it. The tragedy of our world lies in the victimizer's inability to seek forgiveness, and the victims' inability to grant it. We demand justice, but do not demand forgiveness from ourselves. So we repeat the cycle of violence and we teach our children to hate.

> The LORD God has opened my ear
> and I was not rebellious,
> I did not turn backward.
> I gave my back to those who struck me,
> and my cheeks to those who pulled out the beard;
> I did not hide my face
> from insult and spitting.
> The LORD God helps me;
> therefore I have not been disgraced;
> therefore I have set my face like flint,
> and I know that I shall not be put to shame;
> he who vindicates me is near.
> *(Isaiah 50:5–8a)*

The enigma of suffering lies in the fact that it is difficult to justify. Its mystery lies in the revelation that, in God, redemption ensues from it. God does not undo the consequences of our faulty decisions, decisions that make others and us suffer. But God, in all wisdom and power, can come so close to us that though we are suffering, we are graced.

When the Suffering Servant accepts these hard facts, the Suffering Servant walks a thin line between pious yet uncomprehending acceptance of suffering as the "will of God," and angry defiance against an inevitable, though incomprehensible, reality.

The pathology that sometimes mars our religious upbringing begins when we make a simple identification between suffering and God's will. So instead of bearing our suffering –

with the knowledge that though God does not undo it, God nevertheless grants us the courage and the strength to move on – we let suffering bear us down. We drape suffering on ourselves like a mantle of distinction and mistake our lack of discernment for the mark of sanctity. It gets worse when we, in our fiery self-righteousness, brand the "will of God" on others who, at fault or innocent, find themselves already afflicted.

The other pathology is the frenetic attempt to leap out of our skin because our human condition is wedded to suffering. We psychologize everything away and wonder why, after regular trips to the therapist, we are not only financially broke but also still unhappy and unsettled.

The Suffering Servant beholds grace at work, nevertheless. Refusing to either dumbly succumb or blindly escape, the Suffering Servant obeys the prodding of grace, and lives as grace commands.

Though exiled, we can live as grace commands. Though grieving over our loss, we share blessings. Though caught in disjunction, we look out for God's epiphany. In our hope, we assent to God's visitation. Caught in the sway of such grace, we learn to attune ourselves to God's boundlessly self-giving nature. Generosity springs from impoverishment; care from powerlessness; compassion from utter abandonment.

It is in this light that we uncover the centrifugal pull of "Comfort, O comfort my people, says your God." (Isaiah 40:1) We receive God's comfort, and pass it on.

God's comfort cannot be processed, packaged, patented, copyrighted and trademarked only for our private consumption. Its natural exuberance makes of us its living sacrament so that those with whom we come into contact daily may partake of it. To them we proclaim, in word, in presence and in deed, the God of Jeremiah, Ezekiel and Second Isaiah, the God of grief but also of utter, awesome, transcendent holiness, the God of hope but also of suffering servanthood.

In this light, "How can we sing the LORD's song in a foreign land?" (Psalm 137:4) ceases to be about grief. It is about ministering. It asks what we can concretely do for others, recognizing that only from our own pain can we touch their pain. We learn to take very seriously the injunction that we should care for strangers and treat them justly though we are strangers ourselves (Deuteronomy 24:17–19). Though we can glorify ourselves as victims by always putting the blame on others for our suffering, and though we have the right to justice, we can go beyond this, choosing to offer ourselves wholly, like an oblation to this grace that wills to work through us.

We help others see in their own exile a promise of a homecoming in God. We accompany others in their own crisis of upheaval and loss, of dislocation and of hope for a homecoming. We offer a presence that understands and does not offer cheap solutions.

Jeremiah, Ezekiel and Second Isaiah share the exilic condition of God's people. They know loneliness. They know impoverishment. They know deflation of resources. But no one can miss the passionate way they declare God, the Holy One, the Redeemer, the First and the Last, as the only ground for our hope for a homecoming, for justice that lasts, and for personal and structural change. Jeremiah, Ezekiel and Second Isaiah personify God's Suffering Servant. From the underside of history they have remained faithful to the God who says, "Comfort, O comfort my people." (Isaiah 40:1)

We pay homage to Jeremiah, Ezekiel and Second Isaiah. In enlisting them to assist us in interpreting our lives as the exiled have done, we allow them to take us home. And by coming home in God, we too may assume the vocation of suffering servanthood. There are many displaced people in our midst. One can be homeless without leaving home. Because of them, and for the glory of God, we sing the Lord's song in a foreign land.

> See, my servant shall prosper;
> he shall be exalted and lifted up,
> and shall be very high.
> Just as there were many who were astonished at him
> – so marred was his appearance, beyond human semblance,
> and his form beyond that of mortals –
> so he shall startle many nations;
> kings shall shut their mouths because of him;
> for that which had not been told them they shall see,
> and that which they had not heard they shall contemplate.
>
> *(Isaiah 52:13–15)*

As Christians we cannot afford to be coy about how our tradition sees Christ in the Suffering Servant of the LORD. Jesus' prayer in Gethsemane, "My Father, if this cannot pass unless I drink it, your will be done" (Matthew 26:42b), acknowledges, despite his agony, the unmistakable presence of grace like a steady current in murky water. And though that current ineluctably courses through hell, Jesus yields to it. He descends, as our creed declares, and is raised as the Anointed One of God. Jesus hands himself over to sinful humanity, not out of a masochistic love for suffering, but out of a wisdom that knows the indestructibility of God's grace.

The process of prayerfully appropriating exilic theology – the movement from Jeremiah's grief, to being handed over to Ezekiel's valley of dry bones, to envisioning a homecoming in God with Second Isaiah – reveals a process of redemption. Such a process does not cushion us from the blow, but neither does it pretend that suffering is only a frame of mind that adequate therapy can fix. In Isaiah 53, to suffer is to be despised, rejected, held of no account, infirmed, dis-eased, stricken by God, afflicted, wounded, transgressed, crushed, punished, bruised, oppressed, silenced, cut off from the land of the living, pained, anguished, poured out unto death. Yet as long as suffering does not quench our lucidity, as long as it can make us turn to God, we learn to listen to God's own pedagogy of suffering.

Jeremiah teaches us to grieve in God. Ezekiel teaches us to ground all hope in God's holiness. Second Isaiah teaches us to envision homecoming rightly. The will of God is for us to discover the redemptive dimension of suffering. Part of that is also the redemption of the one who causes our suffering.

Redemption in the fourth song of the Suffering Servant has to do with bearing the other's infirmities, iniquities and sins, with carrying the other's dis-eases, with making the other healed and whole, with making one's life an offering for sin, with making many righteous, with interceding for transgressors. The Suffering Servant is a silent lamb led to the slaughter.

Redemption is an active process. When it starts with prayer, we bring our hurts, their surrounding circumstances, and the people involved in them. Even if initially we may want to wish our enemies ill, the ill-wishing gives way to a faith in the power of God's love to remove our fear and our anger if we linger long enough in prayer. The reality of such a love is undeniable. It simply *is*. It has nothing to do with a Hallmark card. It *is*, and it is so true, so good and so beautiful. If we linger longer in this space of prayer, God will flood over us and we will leave prayer with the blessing to act and live as we have prayed. The inspiration to be just is as important as a particular act of justice. The summons to be merciful is embedded in whatever work of mercy we have to perform.

And so let us pray. Again.

A Prayer to Christ, the Suffering Servant of the Lord

Prayerfully place yourself at the juncture in your immigrant life that you find the most difficult to face. Ask Jesus for courage to assume this difficulty totally in his enfolding, surrounding and loving presence. Include everyone who may be involved in your difficulty.

Acknowledge all attendant thoughts and feelings that brood in your consciousness.

Imagining your inner world like Jacob's ladder, on which angels descend and ascend, move down, from your head, down your neck, down your chest, down your stomach, down where you feel the seat of the chair supporting you. Then move up, and as you move slowly, prayerfully, mindfully on each rung, repeat like a mantra this prayer: "Worthy is the Lamb that was slaughtered to receive power and wealth and wisdom and might and honour and glory and blessing!" (Revelation 5:12)

Abide in this space for a while. Trust that instinctively you will know when communing with the Lord achieves its own closure.

Resolve to do something concrete for someone as you continue loving and serving the Lord and others.

A coda for the reader

To be home in God sounds very pious but quite insubstantial. What does that really mean concretely? Is homecoming in God merely theological, that is, merely a shift in the religious imagination? Does it not have an impact on culture – that of the immigrant and of the host country? Does cultural change emerge from an immigrant's growth in faith? These questions are larger than what one life can testify. Though I pose them, I do not have all the answers.

Nevertheless, I suppose that because the biblical tradition has emerged from a particular Semitic culture and has consequently transformed that culture and later other cultures – Greek, Roman, Slavic, Germanic, European, Latin American, African, Asian, etc. – then a similar transformation does happen. How it does so is the next question.

There are certain terms that come to mind if we are to place in context the questions that are raised above: namely, culture, cultural differences, religion and inculturation. Cultural anthropologists and sociologists give them specific meanings, which may come across as quite forbidding, but these meanings actually illuminate very familiar experiences.

When cultural clash became a reality for me, intellectualizing also became a coping mechanism. I needed some theoretical tools to articulate my experience. I needed insights that readers may find quite academic but have helped me to understand, appreciate and respect cultural differences. These insights have made the difficult changes I have faced manageable; in addition, they have enabled me to forgive myself, and also other people when change was just not possible or feasible. These theoretical tools also schooled me to be more observant of cultural peculiarities and more hopeful that as both host culture and immigrants interact, they can indeed create the space in which both can feel at home with each other.

The very emergence of human consciousness coincides with the raising of fundamental questions about the meaning of our existence. Feeling that we may have been thrown into being without our permission, we ask about what exactly is our place in this world. We ask questions about how to organize ourselves effectively so we can curb our tendencies to violence, and survive not apart but together as a community. We ask where we can locate the significance of our life in the flow of time and history. We ask what grants meaning to our own individuality.

Culture is fundamentally a human act of meaning-giving set against the threat of meaninglessness. Predating and outlasting our individual human lives, culture provides us with stability, continuity and security. Culture is objective reality that requires conformity and sustains consistency within the flow of historical events. We even take for granted that culture is just there, like the air we breathe. Only when we lose a sense of it do we start gasping for dear life.

Culture is like quilt-making. It is the fabric on which we sew patches of experiences and relationships in such a way that we can tell our story, and pass this on to the next generation. Outside of the quilt, these discrete patches lose their significance. It is no wonder that loss and disorientation require hope for a homecoming. When our story finds a place in the quilt, we also come home.

Even within one culture, we recognize differences. These differences are more stark in new countries built by immigrants. Geographical location, climate, accidents of history, natural and human resources, and shared temperament may account for why cultures differ from one another. We differentiate Asian culture from Western European from Eastern European, from North American, from African, from Latin American, from Middle Eastern, from West Indian, from Aboriginal and so on.

We can also demarcate cultural differences in terms of East and West, North and South; First, Second, Third, Fourth Worlds; urban and rural; before and after the seventeenth century; before and after the Second World War; pre-modern, modern and post-modern.

Immigrants themselves differ in their ability to integrate. Some measure of negotiation seems to be always at play – a certain kind of give and take that continues until immigrants and host culture forge something new.

We – host country and immigrants – see everything through our cultural glasses. Confrontation with other cultures requires interpretation of both my and the other's culture-laden presumptions and behaviour. One cannot just ask: "What's wrong with *them*?" It is the happy (or unhappy) prerogative of the dominant culture to take itself for granted as the basis for what is and should be. When one becomes an immigrant, that secure standpoint is the first one to be challenged.

Confronted by such a threat, immigrants can be humbled and yet know that they cannot peel off their cultural skin and blinders; or they can huddle in suspicious fear and defensiveness with other like-minded immigrants and dismiss difference as something to subdue; or they can be an open parking lot, taking everything without discernment, wearing the happy smile of the Cheshire cat of *Alice in Wonderland*, while losing their soul.

Similarly, the host country can be humbled by cultural difference while knowing that it cannot cease to be the dominant culture. The host country can be defensive and create its own version of apartheid. Or, it can be so open that it accepts everyone without reasonable scrutiny.

Our – host country's and immigrants' – chosen response either unites or fractures us much more starkly than our countries of origin, or the colour of our skin, or our religious beliefs. Our response to what is different is often instinctive, rather than carefully thought out. Only later do we account for it or rationalize it.

Therefore, part of creating and re-creating a habitable world is listening to and decoding our own and the other's feelings and gut-level reactions. Only then can we cogently account for them. As reason can be unreasonable, we carefully interpret our and the other's cultural response by asking whether our sense of meaning or order is threatened by what is different. We can ask what sense of order we or they are trying to keep. What visceral fear is at issue here? What emotionally satisfying ties are about to be lost?

Cultural change is a result of all these negotiations. When put under the dominating pressure of other cultures, we accommodate, and to a lesser degree both the dominant and other minority cultures also accommodate us. Accommodation can range from that which requires less effort, to that which is more intentional, from what requires cognitive shifts, to what entails emotional allowances, to what exacts gut-level redirection. Arms for warfare, computers, Coca-Cola, McDonalds, Nike, Madonna, and the Backstreet Boys circulate like easy money across the hemisphere. Dim sum, sushi, falafel, souvlaki, yoga, chakra therapy, dream catchers, South African rhythm, sarongs, and Asian rattan furniture co-exist as saleable commodities in metropolitan malls, but their respective elemental undercurrents do not easily transfer over to another culture.

In this uneven terrain, our habitable world stands, complete with linguistic and sub-linguistic categories, deepened by different kinds of emotional undertow, while configuring for us a sense of shared space, shared time, shared rhythm, and shared acknowledgment of the palpably real.

Immigrants may still have to tolerate inconsistencies and move on, knowing that as immigrants, they may never really be deeply rooted in their country of adoption. This new country may be acceptable, but not really home.

The losses and gains in the negotiation are also uneven. The costs are not a matter of arithmetic calculation, but instead involve, according to sociologist Peter Berger, a "calculus of pain, and a calculus of meaning."[7] An outsider looking in should always be prudent about his or her judgments.

When an immigrant prayerfully seeks God as the basis for a homecoming in a foreign land, then religion comes to the fore as a major influence. The whole point of this reflection on the immigrant experience in the light of Scripture is precisely this: that one's faith in God is the beginning of a homecoming.

All religions share the common task of concretizing human self-transcendence in their respective systems and institutions of belief, worship, mores, and community life. From a certain perspective, God or the divine or whatever gives us ultimate meaning is a projection of our desire to outlast death, suffering and evil. The human attempt at world-building will be a tragic and futile exercise without the gift of revelation, without a God who comes to where humans are most exposed, yet also most self-transcending.

It is my conviction that Christianity, and most specifically Roman Catholicism, has wagered on the reliability of divine revelation to respond to our human need for ultimate meaning. By virtue of its belief that God has become human in Jesus, by honouring the most human as the place of divine revelation, Christianity can actually take root in any culture. It is within this perspective that I also believe immigrants who share the same Christian faith can access the biblical theology of exile. Approached in prayer, Jeremiah, Ezekiel and Second Isaiah can transform our religious imagination so that indeed our homecoming may ultimately be rooted in God.

All cultures have a built-in resistance to the good news of salvation, not only for religious reasons, but also for cultural reasons. All cultures have deterrents to religious growth and maturity. All cultures tend to engender their own sets of virtue, as well as their own share of human sinfulness.

As a Christian I believe that all cultures, because of their openness and despite their resistance, will find their ultimate fulfillment in Christ. The theology of creation grants ultimate meaning to our cultural sense of world. The eschatological extends time – past, present, future – to eternity. The love within the Trinity is the ultimate ground for all human loving and relationships. Deep within each one of us is God's image and likeness, the ultimate ground of our sense of self.

I believe that conversion to God is the core of authentic transformation. Change, then, is both change as salvation and interchange among different cultures. Issues of salvation do not only address the question of our relationship with the ultimate but also with each other. As we believe that in God we can outlast what breaks us apart, we can outlast suffering, evil and death, we can also configure a better way to form a human society. Knowing that in God we live forever, we can most securely live within earthly time.

As a Christian I believe that the ultimate, the indestructibly true, good and beautiful, the eternal, the immortal is God, the God of Jesus, the God who is Jesus in the Holy Spirit, the God of Jeremiah, Ezekiel and Second Isaiah. I believe that the salvation offered us does not remove us from our humanity, from our culture, from our particularity. Rather, it begins there in a process of transformation that never ends because love has no end.

Conversion requires constant discernment, but "Greeks do not have to be Jews first, to become Christians." (Acts 15:1–22)

Religious conversion is a challenge for all, individuals and cultures alike. Inculturation, the ongoing process of a culture becoming more transformed by the God of Christ, the God of Jeremiah, Ezekiel and Second Isaiah, is not only for those coming from the Third World. Christianity (or Catholicism) will always have a cultural flavour, but cultural expressions of Catholicism need to be subject to constant purification, and consequently require concrete expression in the life of a faith community.

Despite, therefore, the accidents and sins of history, the cultural disjunctions between my native Filipino culture and the very Spanish and European stamp of sixteenth-century Catholicism that brought Christ to Philippine soils, conversion happens. Conversion takes place right in the mess of cultural domination, acquiescence, compromise, syncretism, power struggle and subjugation.

Catholicism can become a personal choice even if part of it is also imbibing the Greek philosophy behind the creedal tenet that the Holy Spirit proceeds from the Father and the Son, or the scholastic philosophy behind transubstantiation, or the Roman rite behind the official liturgies. I personally do not go so far as to propose that we use the fruit of our land as our Eucharist in the name of inculturation, or eschew everything that is foreign in the attempt to find the face of Christ in my culture.

Catholicism itself becomes the matrix for listening anew to the prophets of exile as they speak not only to an immigrant's experience of displacement but to whoever has a similar experience. For some Catholic immigrants today, listening to the Old Testament prophets may trigger a minor culture shock, but with patience and in prayer, Jeremiah's language of grief, Ezekiel's passion for the holiness of God and Second Isaiah's vision of homecoming may create a revolution in their religious imagination so they, too, can sing the Lord's song in a foreign land.

I admit that I do not have a blueprint about the cultural face of the sense of home of which the prophets of exile speak. The change that results is not merely the crossovers we negotiate across the multicultural plane, but also the call to conversion that confronts us wherever and whenever we cry, "My God, my God, why have you forsaken me?" (Psalm 22:1) Or "How could we sing the Lord's song in a foreign land?" (Psalm 137:4) Should a reader take this construct of the immigrant experience as exile further into his or her life, the story of what God does for humanity continues. Then, with this story embodied in real lives, we will move into the next mystery of our rosary, as it were, or the next pause in the stations of the cross. If, in your own prayerful journey, you meet the God of Jeremiah, Ezekiel and Second Isaiah, please pass the blessing on. "Comfort, O comfort my people, says your God." (Isaiah 40:1)

References

Peter R. Ackroyd. *Exile and Restoration*. Philadelphia: Fortress Press, 1968.

Peter L. Berger. *The Sacred Canopy: Elements of a Sociological Theory of Religion*. New York: Doubleday, 1967.

———. *The Pyramids of Sacrifice: Political Ethics and Social Change*. New York: Basic Books, Inc., Publishers, 1974.

Hervé Carrière, "Inculturaton," in the *Dictionary of Fundamental Theology*, English Language Edition, ed. by René Latourelle. New York: Crossroad, 1995.

Richard J. Clifford. *Fair Spoken and Persuading: An Interpretation of Second Isaiah*. New York: Paulist Press, 1984.

Hadewijch: The Complete Works. Mother Columba Hart, OSB, trans. Classics of Western Spirituality Series. New York: Paulist Press, 1980.

Luke Timothy Johnson. "Imagining the Word Scripture Imagines." *Theology and Scriptural Imagination,* L. Gregory Jones and James J. Buckley, eds. Malden, MA: Blackwell Publishers Ltd., 1998.

George A. F. Knight. *Isaiah 40–55 Servant Theology*. Grand Rapids, MI: Eerdmans, 1984.

Robert Schrieter, CPPS. "Ministry for a Multicultural Church," *Origins* 29, no. 1. May 20, 1999:1, 3–5.

Carroll Stuhlmueller, CP. "Deutero-Isaiah and Trito-Isaiah," in *The New Jerome Biblical Commentary*, Raymond Brown, SS et al., eds. Englewood Cliffs, NJ: Prentice Hall, 1990.

Teresa of Avila. *The Interior Castle*. Kieran Kavanagh, OCD and Otilio Rodriguez, OCD, trans. Classics of Western Spirituality Series. New York: Paulist Press, 1979.

Theological Map of the Immigrant Experience as Exile

Immigrant experience as cycle of loss, disorientation and hope for a homecoming in a foreign land

A PRAYER REFRAIN

Let us pray, as we put ourselves in the presence of God.

Place yourself at the heart of your own experience of loss and disorientation that is mitigated only by hope for healing and redemption. Let us pray:

> *By the rivers of Babylon —*
> *there we sat down and there we wept*
> *when we remembered Zion.*
> *On the willows there we hung up our harps.*
> *For there our captors asked us for songs,*
> *and our tormentors asked for mirth, saying,*
> *"Sing us one of the songs of Zion!"*
> *How could we sing the LORD's song in a foreign land?*
> *(Psalm 137:1-4)*

With immigrants, you are invited to be grateful to their host country, for its hospitality. Let us pray…

With immigrants, you are asked to be forgiving of experiences of racism and discrimination therein. Let us pray…

Consider immigrants from your own ancestral lands, and others who, like them, are suffering from loss and disorientation, and live by a hope of a homecoming in a foreign land. Let us pray…

Carry in your hearts millions and millions of refugees who, right now, are fleeing their homeland: people from Guatemala, El Salvador, Nicaragua, Surinam, Colombia, Haiti; people from Mauritania, Western Sahara, Mali, Senegal, Sierra Leone, Liberia, Togo, Angola, Zaire, South Africa, Mozambique, Burundi, Rwanda, Uganda, Ethioia, Eritrea, Somalia, Sudan, Chad, Zimbabwe; people from Palestine, Iraq, Iran, Tajikistan, Bhutan, Afghanistan; people from Sri Lanka, Cambodia, Indonesia, Laos, Vietnam, Bangladesh, Myanmar, Tibet; people from Yugoslavia, Croatia, Kosovo. Let us pray…

Let us sing our faith: *Only in God will my soul be at rest. From him come my hope and salvation. He alone is my rock of safety, my strength, my glory, my God.*

Dialogue with Scripture within the context of prayer and liturgy—

Jeremiah and the language of grief

Ezekiel and his passion for the holiness of God

Second Isaiah and his vision of a homecoming

Theological self-understanding, and spirituality of the immigrant as exile

Suffering Servant of the LORD as model of ministry

Epilogue

The Theological Map
of the Immigrant Experience
as Exile

On the previous page we find the map of our theological journey with its prayerful anthem.

This prayerful reflection testifies to the need for a kind of praying that carves a hospitable space in the imagination within which immigrants can see their lives and difficulties mirrored without being trivialized. This reflection attempted to speak tenderly about immigrant wounds without creating a defensive posture of victimhood. It paid attention to the ambiguities and ambivalence of culture clash without caricaturing the host country as always being the bad guy. It celebrated the tenacity and daring of immigrants who do gain a secure place for themselves, without glossing over the fact that immigrants can be their own worst enemies.

Crafted largely in solitude, this prayerful reflection remains open to the reality of God. It does not pretend to articulate the economics, politics and sociology of advocating for immigrant rights. It does not offer an incisive analysis of society's propensity to make immigrants out of its own citizens, or the host country's subtle policies of discrimination. It recognizes, but does not comment on, structural sin and justice issues pertaining to immigrants. This prayerful reflection is not a liberation theology of the immigrant experience.

I proclaim the nearness of God. I have faced suffering and grief while also knowing God much more deeply. Not wishing to sidestep the sore points of immigrant life, I do not wish to make a fetish of them either. Rather, I hoped to demonstrate, in the wake of Jeremiah, Ezekiel and Second Isaiah, a graced way of living our immigrant lives in, with and through God, of whom the prophets speak faithfully.

Conceived as a way of addressing radical formational issues of Divine Word College at Epworth, Iowa, this theological cartography has undergone several stages of development in the parish, in academe and in solitude. Though a journey into interiority, it has a strong pastoral thrust and a strong ecclesial dimension. It is a reflection that transfers the skill to whoever receives it as an invitation and a challenge.

A process of spiritual theology

The reflection began with a question: "How can we sing the LORD's song in a foreign land?" (Psalm 137:4) As immigrants, we seek the answer in Scripture. The biblical theology of exile becomes the source for the theological language of our immigrant soul. The fit between experience and biblical theology opens the possibility of a lived spirituality that is at once personal and ecclesial. The next step is the test of shared experience: Does the reflection illuminate further? Does it enchant? Does it capture the imagination? Does it offer possibilities for further enrichment when applied to new situations? Does it open the way for better appropriation?

This reflection takes account of our experience, which, though always multi-faceted, at a certain point becomes essentially religious. Being religious and experiential, the process of reflection enables us to discover our own inner life, which is always replete with possibilities and hazards. There, we existentially know the anguish of "My God, my God, why have you forsaken me?" (Psalm 22:1) or the trust behind "Into your hands I commend my spirit." (Psalm 31:5)

There, the prayerful turn to Scripture occasions a more personal encounter with God, beyond, but carrying over, its mediation through the biblical text. The prayerful turn to Scripture lends ultimate meaning to our experience. Something happens that we call grace.

The witness of Scripture and Tradition points to the fact that if we can speak of God at all, we have to be aware of God's presence, and that this divine presence necessarily affects our consciousness, no matter how subtly. From such awareness ensues the gift of a spirituality that becomes the "home" for continuing reflection. All dimensions of experience are anticipated, and so named, within a biblical world view. The spirituality that develops leads to further reflection. I propose to call this the practice of spiritual theology.

We have engaged in the act of reflecting on the mystery of God in our lives. When we look at our lives in such light, we are theologizing. This reflection is what all ordinary believers do as they recognize the ultimate significance of their lives. Every Christian, then, can theologize.

We cannot engage in theologizing without being practising Christians, without full participation in the lived experience of faith in the community. Spiritual theology is holy wisdom. It is participatory knowledge.

Construing the immigrant experience as exile is one way of doing spiritual theology. It takes us to the threshold of contemplation, making us introspective yet thoroughly biblical, initially solitary but centrally communal, even ecclesial. It implies the activation of consciousness (of mind and heart) but never disembodiment. It emerges as a response to a deep hunger or search for God within an act of loving. It results as a consequence of disciplined effort, yet is always open to grace.

Spiritual theology reckons with the continuous process of self-surrender to God through Jesus in the Holy Spirit. It is a cycle of purgation, illumination and union. In this process we come upon acute disjunctions because we continuously turn from self to God, needing God's grace and being opened by it.

Our experience becomes bearable when seen in the light of the prophets of exile. We own our experience. If we cannot speak about our pain, we will be swallowed up by it. If we do speak, creative forces can surge from deep within and we can overcome. We see signs of life or of transcendence.

We can hand over our powerlessness and "outsider-ness" to the inspiration and power of God's Spirit. We can trust that for the sake of God's holy name, God will declare, "Dry bones…you shall live!" (Ezekiel 37:4–6) Such assurance does not drug us into slumber. Instead, it invites us to entrust our anxious wakefulness into a kind of peace that only God can give. Still experiencing an impasse in which we face an ebbing of resources, of energy, of possibilities, and still confronting the temptation to cynicism, despair and disenchantment, we nevertheless risk the faith that God's inscrutable presence will hold us aloft in faith, hope and love.

Spiritual theology demonstrates Bernard Lonergan's precepts: "Be attentive; be intelligent; be reasonable; be responsible; and be loving."[8] Attentiveness focuses on the whole spectrum of what we experience, including contemplation. Intelligence names, understands, makes connections, critiques, analyzes and synthesizes everything into some meaningful whole. Reasonableness discerns whether what is claimed is cogent, coherent, consistent, true and adequate to reality. Responsibility impels us to live and act according to what we see as true, good and beautiful. The decision to love follows.

We begin with attentiveness to the cycle of loss, of disorientation, and of hope for a homecoming. We name the experience and articulate its religious dimension. We dialogue with Scripture. We articulate our predicament as exile. We discover its potential for ministry patterned after the vocation of the Suffering Servant of the LORD. We cannot be suffering servant for the LORD apart from the grace of love.

A spiritual theology that is also a pedagogy

The process towards naming the immigrant experience as exile cannot be divorced from the construct itself. Demonstrating its transferability to other similar experiences makes clear that this process of reflection is also an educational event. Our concrete experience meets biblical theology, and results in ministry. We integrate rationality and affectivity, the autobiographical and the ecclesial, the liturgical and the ministerial, the biblical and the experiential, the historical and the eschatological.

We can call this a pedagogy of creative appropriation. As in any process of education, the inherent pedagogy brings together five elements at once: text, process, learner, teacher and learning environment. The key text is the biblical theology of exile. The process of communication is the prayerful encounter between experience and Word of God that requires our psychological readiness and our willingness to be drawn into prayer. Within prayer we confront our own experience, which enables us to receive God's Word. We go beyond naive appreciation of Scripture, without becoming overly critical exegetes.

The quality of encounter between biblical text and human experience, as well as our encounter with one another, is dependent on the manner in which the Word is proclaimed, our openness to our own experience, the trust that is nurtured in the dialogue, and the establishment of an environment that makes prayer and therefore appropriation possible.

The pedagogy is a form of midwifery in that it helps us not only to come to terms with our experience, but also to transform our experience as the ground for reflection and for personalizing the drama of salvation history – from call to exodus, wandering in the desert, covenant, nationhood, prophecy, waiting in exile, and to vocation as Suffering Servant of the LORD.

Praying provides the comfort zone for listening to all aspects of our experience. There may be moments of recognition when the biblical text verbalizes our otherwise unspoken or even unrecognized emotions: our pain, our grief, our anger, our cry in the night, our anguish, our hope, our patience, our trust.

Praying presupposes that we listen to the Word within a faith community that celebrates the Word in liturgy. Scripture reveals the God of Christianity continually at work within human and cosmic history. Human experience is ultimately consecrated to be the place for an encounter with God. It has interpenetrating dimensions that always need articulation. And Scripture has an excess of meaning that is offered for appropriation. Shedding light on the immigrant experience, Scripture nuances it with religious significance.

The pedagogy initiates us into a lifetime apprenticeship in the craft called theologizing. From within our own state of need we take a leap of faith. An implosion into doubt would be suicide. This theological enterprise takes place within a religious commitment, within a horizon of faith, in close bonds with prayer, worship and ministry. We are not detached from, but are dwelling in, faith. Dwelling therein grants us a kind of knowledge from the inside, an ecclesial instinct, a sense of faith.

The pedagogy in theologizing is also a pedagogy in contemplation. Theologizing is praying. In the *lectio divina,* we gather all that we are in the presence of God. We acknowledge God as the Holy One. We listen and respond to God. We say "Amen." These foundational, prayerful acts, which are also liturgical, engage our being. In doing them, we acknowledge who we are before God, mentally, affectively and viscerally. The dynamics of listening and responding move from the prosaic, to the symbolic, to the ineffable. "Amen" is intoned in word and in silence.

Contemplation requires full engagement and commitment. Its fruit is shown in the signs of conversion that flow out into worship and ministry. Contemplation is a part of creative appropriation. It is creative because it involves informative and, more important, committed and transformative knowledge. One cannot be an outsider looking in. One has to wrestle not only with the immigrant experience but also with the Word of God.

The pedagogy of creative appropriation also involves imbibing a biblical imagination, an imagination that takes as a paradigm the essential dynamic and content of God's story with God's people as recorded in Scripture, and lived within their ongoing Tradition. The allegorical, moral and anagogical reading of Scripture is a series of imaginative leaps that enable Jeremiah, Ezekiel and Second Isaiah to come to life here and now, thereby giving us fuller life. Their penetrating insight into the human condition, as well as their unwavering, though tested, faith in God, become the very prism through which our own predicament can be read and brought to redemption. They offer us a language for our soul that includes even what we cannot articulate. They offer us a host of images that will help tame the terrors of the yet unknown. As we let them into our world, they in turn invite us to inhabit theirs. And as we do, we behold the glory of God.

The biblical theology of exile has a much wider application than is demonstrated within the purview of the immigrant experience. But as appropriated by the immigrant, this theological construct has a prophetic potential to speak to the Church and to the world, calling us to be engaged. Our theologizing is not just a way of *doing* but also a way of *being*.

A spirituality of exile

We nurture an exilic spirituality at the heart of paradox. We are caught in the paradox of home and homelessness. A certain kind of loneliness accompanies this in-between state. We grieve after the loss of home, and grieve for a sought-after home. We come to terms with this grief only with the realization that such grief is also God's grief, and that God's holiness is the only sure ground for a hope of a homecoming.

In-betweenness generates a strong sense of pilgrimage. Once we are uprooted, our rerooting elsewhere will not be as deep or as firm. A sense of contingency and tenuousness imprints upon our soul. The Israelites wandered in the desert and learned to pitch their tents temporarily whenever and wherever tiredness overcame them, whenever and wherever there was some sign of safety from desert marauders and some source of food and drink. We can only move forward beyond the nostalgia for what once was, and the strangeness of the now. A sense of pilgrimage is part of our exilic self-understanding. We are a pilgrim people.

A sense of pilgrimage makes us learn to befriend greyness – the flat, routine, boring, day-to-day, undramatic region between our clear memories of home, the imposing reality of our adopted land and the darkness of the unknown. The crisis of upheaval and loss is pushed far back in our minds The crisis of disorientation becomes familiar. It no longer surprises us. We get used to it.

We do more than simply adapt to the unalterable facts of our situation, more than just tolerate an unpleasant condition. We do not keep tensing up in the face of a dull, numbing pain that will not go away. We value this greyness because within this awkward place we call on the LORD, we pray, we keep watch. The sense of isolation that we experience in keeping watch is very much like the isolation of the exilic prophets as they accompany God's people to and from exile, towards a homecoming.

Greyness also means silence. Both accompany waiting. We wait for God to come and to help us make sense of our own crises, even if oftentimes we wonder whether our state is not merely some form of inertia or paralysis. Can we really wait for God here? Does God want us to wait? Or are we perhaps missing something? Yet to jump out of greyness into activities that might consume our energy can feel like a betrayal of our calling. God calls us to this exilic place for reasons that will only be clear in the future. Befriending greyness makes sense in the context of waiting for God to make God's promises come true. The greyness is where we await the dawn.

Vigilance for here and hereafter sustains waiting. We must be very pragmatic in terms of survival. We do not have the luxury to pine for what has been or what is yet to be. We can only hope. The business of daily living demands our total attention. Yet we vigilantly keep our hope alive. Suspicious of solutions that are too facile or too glib, we dare trust that our exilic state is itself a state of grace. So in its pull we become attentive not only to our needs, but, more especially, to the needs of others. We can be open to ministry, which includes the paradox of involvement and detachment: we become contemplative in a world of action. Action, ministry and service demand involvement. Contemplation, praying in the night, entails detachment.

Involvement signifies that we do not have the luxury of taking a "flight into the desert." No refuge remains. We find ourselves in the fray of life, as individuals and as Church. Yet the hunger for home sets us apart from the fray. There will always remain this ache in our hearts, a cry in the dark for God to come anew.

So we keep the old while awaiting the radically new. We recognize the graced dimension of powerlessness as we learn the art of humble waiting. Our destiny is not totally in our hands, yet we dispose ourselves wholly for God to work in us.

Our immigrant life educates us to withstand instability and tenuousness. We learn to cherish what we have after losing so much. And we can never be fooled into presuming that whatever we cherish will not be lost again.

We dwell in the gift of a biblical imagination. Like the Deuteronomist and the custodians of the priestly tradition, who reread the story of their ancestors in the light of the exilic experience, we can see our condition as being like Noah's, keeping intact the basics of communal survival amidst the flood of circumstances beyond our control. We occupy the Tower of Babel, unable to assert our own meaning over the cacophony of meanings, yet at the same time, unable to give up what we believe to be true. Biblical insights remain valid and illuminating in our contemporary existence.

The hoped-for homecoming may take a long time, but the immigrant as exiled person has been schooled to wait, to work within an eschatological understanding of Christian existence: salvation is now, but not yet consummated. The immigrant as exile is busy being totally present to the here and now while remaining vigilant for what is to come.

Our theologizing takes on a strong communal dimension when praying through our immigrant experience makes us conscious of others with whom we create a habitable world in the region of in-betweenness. We also acknowledge those in our midst who are of the dominant Anglo-Saxon-based Canadian culture, French-Canadian culture and the Native peoples, who feel as marginalized or as in-between as we do because there are just too many of us dismantling their sense of world.

There is also a marked ecclesial significance to this theologizing. The Church is in its own exile. Marginalized because of its religious commitments as well as by the burdens of its sins of the past and of the present, it can turn to the prophets of exile and, in prayer, await new things from the God who always wants to save.

Exile – geographical, existential, spiritual, theological, ecclesial – is the threshold for divine revelation. Stripped bare by our loss, we wring out of ourselves an elemental cry for God. Grieving utters as prayer what would have been otherwise muffled by other desires and pretensions. Disoriented by failed expectations about how life should be, we are oriented to await an epiphany of the Holy One, our God. Drawn into God's circle of grace, we become God's call for others to come home.

These five sentences frame the story of how we can meet God, no matter our particular circumstance. Five simple sentences can bring forth a rush of expectations that can transform into hope. Between the lines, prophetic image after prophetic image will captivate our imagination. These images speak volumes about what God has done and will continue to do if we so allow God to take us home.

References

Avery Dulles. *The Craft of Theology: From Symbol to System.* New York: Crossroad, 1992.

Bernard J. F. Lonergan, SJ. *Method in Theology.* New York: Herder and Herder, 1972.

Notes

[1] The prayerful reflection on the immigrant experience as presented in these pages is applicable only to first-generation immigrants. Subsequent generations will have to find their own way towards appropriation of the biblical theology of exile should they, and others like them, also find themselves on the shifting sands of displacement and homelessness.

[2] The seeds for this book were sown in an article I wrote entitled "How Can I Sing God's Song in a Foreign Land: Immigrant Experience as Exile," which was published in *New Theology Review*, vol. 12, no. 1 (February 1999):25–31.

[3] Eugene Ehrlich, *Amo, Amas, Amat and More* (New York: Harper and Row, Publishers, 1985), 104.

[4] If Jeremiah bought a field in an occupied territory, he expressed the conviction that one day, past the time of exile, he could use it. This was an expression of his faith and hope in God. The other exiles could imitate him. See *The New Jerome Biblical Commentary*.

[5] See *The Shorter Oxford English Dictionary on Historical Principles,* Third Edition (London: Oxford University Press, 1973).

[6] Refrain of "Holy Darkness," copyright 1988, 1989 by Daniel L. Schutte and the North American Liturgy Resources (NALR), 10802 North 23rd Avenue, Phoenix, Arizona, 85029.

[7] Peter L. Berger, *The Pyramids of Sacrifice: Political Ethics and Social Change* (New York: Basic Books, 1974), xiii.

[8] Bernard J.F. Lonergan, *Method in Theology* (New York: Herder and Herder, 1972).